THROUGH A PIGSKIN PRISM

AN UNLIKELY JOURNEY
TO AND THROUGH THE NFL

E. BLAKE MOORE JR.

DENVER, COLORADO

Through a Pigskin Prism
An Unlikely Journey to and through the NFL
All Rights Reserved.
Copyright © 2014 E. Blake Moore Jr.
v3.0

Outskirts Press, Inc.
http://www.outskirtspress.com

ISBN: 978-1-4787-3613-4

Library of Congress Control Number: 2014911990

Outskirts Press and the "OP" logo are trademarks belonging to Outskirts Press, Inc.

PRINTED IN THE UNITED STATES OF AMERICA

*To my wife, Cynthia Weiler, whose love,
understanding, and patience have sustained me
through much of my life journey.*

*To my children, Lauren and Hudson,
who have brought immeasurable joy to my life.*

Contents

Introduction

I THINK AN introduction to any book should address two basic questions: First, what is the book about? Second, why did the author choose to write it?

The first question seems easy to answer—this is a book about my "football career," the story of my years as a football player, my football memoirs. But the more I wrote, the more I realized how apt the title of the book is. For my football story is really a very small part of my overall life, yet it also permeates so many other parts of my life that it is hard to separate football from "other." In fact, as I wrote the book, I realized that even in telling the football story, I was only telling a small part of my life—because there are just so many memories, so many emotions, so many connections to things "outside" football. So I had to make choices about what I wrote, which stories to include, which to omit. Some of the names have been changed where I thought appropriate. And I am not under any illusion that I have every story perfectly accurate, or that others who were part of my life would remember it as I have remembered it. Such is history and human observation. I have taken time to try to get the "facts" right, like games, scores, dates, etc. But the stories—those are mine, and I relate them as I remember them.

The second question—why write the book—is perhaps more complicated. Over the years, as I have told bits and pieces of my football story to one or two people, or to groups or audiences, I have often heard the remark—"You have a fascinating story—You should write a book!" I brushed the remark off for many years, but kept hearing it as I related my story to different people. The interest seemed persistent and genuine. I guess we'll see how many people were serious after I publish . . .

I am also writing this book for my children, Lauren and Hudson. They were far too young while I was playing to really understand what I was doing, or what it meant. I was just their dad. As they've grown older, I think they have a better sense of what their dad did, but never really understood the whole story, start to finish. So part of the "why" is for them.

Finally, and probably more urgently of late, is mortality. I have written most of this book, the guts of it, during 2011–2013, at age 55 or so. In that brief period of time, the issue of head trauma in the NFL, the consequences of all those blows to the head over a long high school, college, and NFL career, have become a national health debate and controversy. My NFL peers are dying, experiencing early onset dementia and committing suicide. None of those topics were ever discussed even 10 years ago by me or other former players. Our health concerns were always physical—weight, joints, pain. None of us ever imagined there was a silent mental killer out there waiting for us too. Now we know. And I want to tell my story, the way I remember it, before I forget.

Preface

I'M CROUCHED OVER the football, left fingers on the Astroturf, right hand grasping the ball, prepared to snap it through my legs to the waiting quarterback. Sweat is running down my face, off my head, under my helmet. My tee shirt is soaked with sweat mixed with blood from my shoulders. Across from me is one Rod Horn, #71, the pride of Nebraska, nose tackle, 270 pounds of beef-fed, all-American Cornhusker. Rod is a high third-round pick in the draft for the Cincinnati Bengals, and he is convinced that he will either make the team, or not, based on the ass-whipping he puts on me on this very play.

We are equipped with helmets, shorts, T-shirts, and pressure at this first Cincinnati Bengals minicamp for all the new rookies, and a few veterans who barely made the team last year. It's an early but warm spring day in a blighted downtown area of the city. The practice facility has grass and turf practice fields, a parking lot, and a low cinder block building surrounded by fences. At this first minicamp, we rookies are supposed to demonstrate our athletic skills and conditioning for the coaching staff while running through plays and drills over the course of a long weekend. That meant about 12 draft picks, with future Hall of Famer and #1 draft pick Anthony Munoz the most notable, and several other "free agents" like me, signed by the team to round out the group and fill empty practice spots.

The QB yells "Blue 19, blue 19. Hut! Hut!" I snap the ball and fire out to meet Mr. Nebraska. Rod, apparently, failed to note our attire (no pads) and that this was a "noncontact" drill. For the twentieth time that practice, he head butted me on the shoulders with his face mask, jammed his meaty paws into my chest, throat, face—whatever was available—and went full speed until the whistle blew. More blood seeped from my now-raw shoulders. I went back to the huddle to get ready for the next play. I was the only center in minicamp. Rod was the only nose tackle. It was going to be a long weekend . . .

What the hell was I doing here . . .?

Just a Kid

I WAS BORN in 1958 in Durham, North Carolina, while my dad was in his third year of law school at Duke. My mom was a UNC grad. I weighed in at around 8–9 pounds at birth, a pretty healthy boy. Not sure how my petite, 5 foot 5 inch mom pulled that off.

We moved while I was a few weeks old to Chattanooga, Tennessee. My dad took a job as a lawyer for a small but quality law firm there, a firm he stayed with for 46 years until his retirement. He was 6 feet tall, broad shouldered, and well-built, but not big. There was nothing really in my genetic history to suggest I might someday be an NFL offensive lineman. Sure, my great-grandfather played football for the 1889 Wooster University team—no helmets—and they beat the same team twice that year for a perfect 2-0 record. And my grandfather was a trackman at said Wooster University, and yes, my dad did play center at the (same) College of Wooster for his intramural touch football team. And my mom was quite athletic, though when young she was limited (by social stereotype) to cheerleading. Nevertheless, I am convinced it is her competitive gene that I inherited, and that drove me relentlessly.

I don't recall playing any organized sports really until fourth grade or so. Until then, growing up in Chattanooga, I basically played hard at recess. I played informal touch and tackle football or basketball games whenever we could get enough kids together to play, whether at school or after school. The "organized" sports in early grade school tended to be kickball, dodgeball, softball, or "Red Rover." The latter was played by forming up two teams lined up across from one another, about 20 yards apart, arms linked. One team would yell at the other: "Red Rover, Red Rover, send Blake (for example) on over," at which point I would run full speed at the weakest point in their line and attempt to break through. Given I was one of the beefier kids, once I got my momentum up, I was tough to stop. Breaking through meant the runner continued playing; failing to break through and you're out.

In the summertime I was sent to "day camp," which I now know was a way for my mom to get a break from an extremely active boy. For me, it was a chance to play all day, from tag to archery to kickball to just about anything the camp counselors could think up to keep us busy (and tired!).

All this time I continued to grow and was usually one of the larger kids in my class, but not the biggest, and certainly not the most gifted athletically. What I lacked in athletic skill I tried to make up for in enthusiasm. Really, I was one of any of hundreds, thousands, of rather chunky grade-school kids you can see at schools every day. But I always thought, even then, I could play, and win, any game I tried. I was a fierce competitor and hated to lose—a race, a game, ping pong, Red Rover—or in the classroom. My competitive nature applied to my grades and schoolwork too. I always believed I should be the best in class, and loved to be #1.

I attended a small private school, The Bright School (not a play on words, but named for the founders), and in grades 1–6 we moved through school with pretty much the same group of kids. The grade competition could be intense (well, for me), and I was always trying to score higher than the smartest person in my class, Janet Zuckerman. Sometimes I managed, but she was tough on the (chalk)boards!

My earliest recollection of organized football was something we called "GraY," pronounced "gray-y," as two words. It was a youth football program organized by the YMCA, though we formed teams with our school classmates. It was flag football—no tackling or helmets or pads. In fact, I don't recall any youth football program that involved pads and contact. No Pop Warner around back in the late '60s that I remember, in the South anyway. And in the South in the '60s and '70s, there was FOOTBALL, and then all the other sports. Sure, I played basketball, wrestled ("wrassled," as we said in the South), and some baseball too. But football—Football—it was king, number one. You played football if you were an athlete. You played all the other sports if you had time after football.

My memory is a bit hazy as to whether we started our Bright School GraY flag football team in fourth or fifth grade, but pretty sure it was fourth grade. We would usually practice a couple times a week after school, red and yellow plastic flags velcroed and fluttering from our hips. Bigger, slower guys to the line—offense and defense. Smaller, faster guys playing in the backfield or quarterback or receiver, and defensive backs on defense. Of course, that landed me on the line, both offense and defense. Still large and a good layer of boyish fat, freckles, a mop of brown hair, and a red face after running, I could run but never fast enough to be one of the elite speedsters in my class. The fastest kid in our class at Bright School was a redheaded squirt named Stevie. I think he had braces the whole time I knew him. There were some other fast kids a little bigger, but in flag football, it is all about speed. And Stevie was fast!

Well, speed and deception. We really didn't throw the football much in our GraY league. Remember, this was the time of Jim Brown and other NFL running back greats. Paul Brown had yet to revolutionize the NFL with the forward pass. It was a ground game, and that is how we played it. The bread-and-butter play was the sweep—toss the ball back to Stevie or some other fast kid, we offensive linemen would try to block for a second or two, and then hopefully Stevie would get someone to miss and go streaking down the sideline.

Next level of sophistication: the single reverse. Start the sweep to the right, and then hand the ball off to another back coming to the left. Often that would create large open areas of running room, because, remember, for most 10–12-year-olds, once you commit to one direction, it is hard to go back. Once we had the single reverse working, and the other team was starting to figure that out: of course . . . the double reverse.

Now, you can imagine that, at 12-year-old speed, these plays could take quite a while to develop. Start the sweep right, hand the ball to the guy coming back to the left, and now hand it again to someone coming back the original direction, to the right. We linemen would sort of block one way for a bit, then another way, but usually after the first couple seconds, we would simply watch the play to see if Stevie would break loose. ("Blocking" at this level basically meant bumping into anyone I could, with my chest or shoulder.)

The ultimate level of deception in flag football was the dreaded triple reverse. That's right—sweep right, back left, back right, then back left. At our speed, I think it took 10 seconds for all that to happen. The other team's coach would be yelling "Reverse! Reverse!" but hell, what good did that do them? Reverse which way? How many? Ultimately, the best defensive strategy against the triple reverse was to just stand still for a while—the guy with the ball would be back by, eventually. Of course, though, that didn't work too well if it was just a sweep, in which case just standing there didn't produce very good defensive results.

So you get the gist of our high-scoring offense. We confused the hell out of the other teams and usually scored lots of touchdowns. And we had enough fast guys on defense to stop the other teams, who never really seemed to manage offenses as "sophisticated" as ours. The results over the grade-school years fourth through sixth—we won every game we played. Until one of the last games of sixth grade.

As noted, I was growing up in Chattanooga, Tennessee, in the '60s. And in the '60s in Chattanooga, that meant race issues and segregation were still realities in a very real and raw way. Bright School, private, was as white as the driven snow in those days. That was not unusual at the time—many schools, private and public, were either all-white or all-black. Separate but equal. Not.

My parents were both raised on, and preached, the truth of equality, and reinforced that in action. Part of my required reading while young: Martin Luther King's biography and Malcolm X's biography. Many lectures on right and wrong. And a personal example that has always stuck with me. At Bright School we had a janitor, and though I can't remember his name, I *do* remember him. I will call him Jim Elder. He was probably in his 50s or 60s, black, and had been working at The Bright School for many years, mopping, sweeping, and generally cleaning up after a lot of white kids in a private school. He did his job with a quiet dignity. Kids would address him by his first name, as if he were an equal. When my dad heard about this, and I think I was in third or fourth grade, he told me that calling this man by his first name was not respectful—we kids would *never* be allowed to refer to an older *white* man by his first name. My instruction from my dad, in a lesson I never forgot, was to apologize to Mr. Elder. So next time I saw him cleaning in the hall, I, a 10- or 11-year-old, screwed up my courage to apologize to him for using his first name. He, of course, said it was fine, no problem, but from then on, in front of my classmates, I always greeted him as Mr. Elder. He said it didn't matter, but I think my dad was right—it *did* matter.

Why did I bring this up now? Back to that last flag football game, in sixth grade. We as a class had *never* lost a game. We simply knew we were the best. That last game, we were playing a team from one of the "desegregated-but-somehow-still-all-black" schools. They were good, and they were fast. We couldn't score. The reverses didn't work on them. They couldn't score either, until they finally did manage a touchdown sometime late in the game. We had another chance to score, and in my memory, we *did* score, only to have it called back by the referee for a penalty that we sixth graders just *knew* was unjustified. But there it was, painfully, our only loss as a class team in three years, to a team entirely different from ours in so many ways. We were terribly upset. Looking back, for me, it was also another lesson in respect and equality.

By the time I left The Bright School in 1970, I was a husky, active, smart boy who loved playing football, watched it on TV, read about it in *Sports Illustrated*, and cheered on the Minnesota Vikings (I liked the "Purple People Eaters" of the Vikings). I was blissfully growing up in what I thought was a stable family with two good parents and two little brothers (5 and 10 years younger). I had applied for and would be attending one of the two best private schools in Chattanooga—The Baylor School. My life was school, sports, football, church every Sunday, and playing with friends. And playing with friends meant pickup games, bikes, rock climbing, and all manner of outdoor active play. No video games in those days, and really, TV reception was limited to two pretty good signals—both network, of course. So other than Saturday morning cartoons (before sports action), and *Gunsmoke*, and NFL on Sundays, not much to keep a boy indoors.

I know now, of course, that while my life was seemingly calm and blissful, that society as a whole was going through fundamental and radical changes—Vietnam, Kent State, birth control, civil rights, protests, busing, George Wallace, race riots. But my life was simple. Or so I thought . . .

CHAPTER 2

Junior High School (1970–1973)

THE BAYLOR SCHOOL. Actually, in 1970, it was The Baylor School for Boys. And a military academy (not uncommon in the South at that time—the other fine private boys' school was McCallie—also then a military academy). Many of my Bright School classmates, of course, also went with me to Baylor. It was the natural progression of schooling for middle-class/upper-class white boys at the time. (The girls went to GPS—Girls' Preparatory School.) Even though attending with many of my grade-school friends, arriving at Baylor as a 12-year-old seventh grader, getting outfitted in full military uniform, from the army-type hat with a shiny black bill, down to the spit-shined black dress shoes, and heavy wool jacket to be worn with medals and pins—was pretty intimidating. We were organized into platoons, learned to march in step, took orders from upperclassmen ("officers"), and shuddered at the thought that we might be called out for a smudge on our shoe, a tie tied improperly, or failing to quickly obey a command from one of those intimidating seniors. I was scared as hell—and I wasn't alone.

But we were Baylor Boys—so we sucked it up, learned the system, took our orders, shined our shoes, and kowtowed to the up-perclassmen. When we weren't in class or on parade, we were still seventh-grade boys running around, going to school, aggravating our teachers. Of course, I signed up to play football—seventh-grade team. Football was so popular that there was actually a team for the seventh grade alone. All my buddies from Bright School signed up too, of course. And our adventure was now the *real* thing: tackle football.

For pretty much all of us, this was the first time to ever put on pads, a full football uniform. We were going to start playing the game we had been imitating for so long. None of us knew how to even put on our pads. They basically handed us our pants, pads, shoulder pads, and a helmet. Size the helmet? Barely. Didn't matter much—it was literally a thin plastic shell with a few nylon "suspension" straps inside it, theoretically to help suppress the blows about to come. When I tried to figure out how to put the knee pads and thigh pads into the special pouches designed for them, I managed to get the thigh pads in the wrong way so that one wrong move could have pinched off a rather important part of my anatomy. Fortunately at that age the size, and thus the risk, were minimal.

Once all of us had sort of figured out which pads went where and how to put on a helmet, we headed out to practice where we would, for the first time, learn to hit someone, and *be* hit by someone. It was a hot August day, steamy hot, next to the Tennessee River. We gathered around as the coach explained our first drill: bull in the ring. This would be my first experience with football drills that somehow always lived up to their names (we'll address the "nutcracker" later). The coach organized us into groups of about eight players. He handed everyone a padded blocking dummy to hold and told us to form a small circle. He then told one of us to put down the blocking dummy and get in the middle of the circle. When he called the name of a player in the circle, his job was to run into the player in the center of the circle, the "bull," with the blocking dummy, as hard as he could. The bull was supposed to quickly turn and meet his attacker, with authority. The drill commenced. Frank—wham; Vince—wham; Jeff—wham; wham wham wham.

The coach called out names from the ring with increasing speed, usually until the bull in the ring had been flattened at least once. Fun drill for the guys with the blocking dummies. Not so much fun for the bull. I took my first turn as the bull, had my first contact as a football player in pads. Before long, the dummies were coming at me too fast—I was getting pummeled, knocked around, hit to the ground. I didn't give up—I don't give up easily—but I did start crying angry, mad tears. Sweat, slobber, tears all mixed together. I got mad. I fought back through my tears. And that actually gave me strength and determination. I always feel like that bull-in-the-ring drill was my initiation into "real" football. I realized then and there that you better be ready to take the punishment . . . and give it out. And I never cried in practice again.

Seventh grade seemed like a blur of gray military uniforms, shiny shoes, parade and formation marching, and really tough teachers. Being a military academy, many of the teachers were former military men. Colonel Watson. Major Worsham. Sarge. Yeah, just Sarge—not sure I ever knew his last name. He was "Sarge." These guys were tough and made sure we runts knew it. All teachers were addressed formally, by title and last name. Major Worsham. Never "Mr." Unless you weren't military, then it was Dr. or Mr. or whatever. And we were called by our last names only: "Moore, get over here!" or "Aiken, what are you doing there?!" "Trundle, put that eraser down." Discipline was strict. You didn't even *think* about being late to class. No one wanted Major Worsham or Colonel Watson glaring at you, in full dress uniforms, medals all over their chests and shoulders, while you skulked in late to class.

I remember Colonel Watson well for seventh-grade geography. Yes, he taught geography—and with a vengeance. No country too small, no capital city to be unknown. Forgot to write your name on your quiz? Minus 10 points. He could ask for any mountain range on any continent and you'd better damn well know it. Rockies? Alps? Appalachians? Child's play. How about the Urals? Wasatch? Caucasus? Our final exam was memorable, and we even were told what it would be before arriving in class: draw a map of (1971) Africa, with *every* country and capital. Terrifying! I still remember one capital at that time was Ouagadougou. Seriously.

We seventh-graders persevered. Survived the discipline,

last-minute inspections, daily shoe polishings, and upperclassmen brown-nosing ("Yes sir, Mr. Paden, sir!"). And at the end of every fall day we got to get out of the military uniforms and into our football gear. Hard to believe, but much more comfortable.

I was one of the larger kids on the team (read: stocky and slow), and so I was naturally assigned to the line. Played tackle on offense and on defense. We still played both ways in those days, and it was great to play on the defensive side. Loved going after the ball and making tackles. On offense there was more structure, and it was hard to block the other guy. The blocking technique at the time basically involved holding your fists in at your chest, sticking your elbows up and out, and aiming your face mask at the defender, hoping you'd hit him momentarily with something. This proved pretty hard to do. So, defense was "fun," offense was hard.

Our offense was basically sweep left, sweep right, run it up the middle. Repeat. Passes were an anomaly. Even so, we seventh-grade Baylor Red Raiders were dominant. No one could touch us, and we went undefeated as a seventh-grade team, 7-0 or 8-0. No close games. We were so far ahead in one game that the coach actually called the tackle eligible (pass play) for me! I was supposed to run a "banana route" (see, very sophisticated), which meant when the ball was snapped, I was to "peel" out a few yards and catch the pass. Ball hit me somewhere at knee level, incomplete, receiving career over (apparently . . .). Baylor Red Raiders—seventh-graders—undefeated! And, of course, most importantly, we kicked the ass of our archrival, McCallie.

I finished up seventh grade on the "distinguished list" academically—straight As. Figured out how to make two uniforms last a full week (they were expensive) and how to keep my shoes semi-shiny with minimal effort (saliva was involved). I had my teammates, classmates, friends at a great school, where I thought I'd be through high school. Little did I know, my world was about to change.

I mentioned this was a time of significant civil turmoil and racial unrest, particularly in the South. I had been largely insulated from that. Not a single black classmate from the time I started school through seventh grade. There was also a big debate about the "privileged" kids getting to go to private high schools like Baylor, which were not only all-white, but also expensive and, at the time, military. My dad was passionate about equal rights, civil rights, class distinctions, and had been raised in an extremely liberal family of educators. He finally, I think, could not justify in his own mind why his son (me) should be entitled to go to Baylor, when so many other kids had no choice other than the public school system. A system that was, by most standards, struggling at the time. Result? I was told that in eighth grade, I would be leaving Baylor, my friends, my classmates, my team—and attending Signal Mountain Junior High School.

Where?

August 1971. My mom drove me slowly into the empty parking lot at Signal Mountain Junior High. The junior high school was about 30 minutes from where we lived. It was a hot August day. No one else was around. When my mom was involved, being early and first to arrive was part of the program. I think she was crying. She was never a big fan of pulling me out of Baylor. She wanted the best for her sons, and she was sure this wasn't the best. I got out, climbed into the small aluminum bleachers at one end of the parking lot, and waited as my mom drove away.

My new teammates, and classmates, and eventually friends, began to arrive. I did not know a single person, and none of them would know me. Some were dropped off by moms and dads, like me. A few others arrived on their motorbikes, which, I guess in Tennessee at the time, was OK for a 15-year-old (the ninth-graders). Many of them looked 18 or 20 to me—I was still a prepubescent chubby boy, about 5 foot 10, maybe 160 pounds. Good lineman material. Pretty soon we were all assembled, with some shy hellos by me. Most of these guys knew each other and had been together on Signal Mountain since first grade—kind of like my friends at Baylor *used* to be for me. I was alone.

Our coach soon arrived. Al Ball. Ex-marine, I think; buzz haircut, stocky, tending to overweight. Turns out he was also the physical education teacher at the school. Coach Ball was a believer in toughness and discipline, and with this group of teenage boys, that was probably exactly what the doctor ordered.

As the phys ed teacher, I would later learn, he was also the one teacher at the school who wielded a paddle for punishment. That's right, a good-sized oak paddle which was applied when necessary. And "when necessary" could be anything from talking in class to throwing things in class to fighting in class (remember, this was junior high). The punishment would come in the way of "licks"; i.e., three licks for one crime or five licks for another. And they hurt. Coach Ball was a master of the paddle, and exactly where he chose to apply the paddle had a lot to do with how much it hurt. Smack on the butt— bad but not too bad. Down lower on the hamstrings—now that really hurt. And if he *really* wanted to make a point, he would take out the paddle with holes drilled in it—a specialty model. The holes intensified the pain—very scientific. I had a few licks in my junior high days, but I usually behaved well enough to avoid them.

I digress. Coach Ball had our small group of football players there at SMJH. It was a rough bunch. Some would be described by my former Baylor friends as "country," or "hicks," or worse. But this was my new world, and these were the first people I met at SMJH and would be my team. There was never a moment where I considered not playing football—it was one of the things I did. I showed up every day dutifully for my thrashing at the hands of the ninth-graders. We put on our primitive pads and helmets, old/used pants, and strapped the "hip girdle" pads around our waist which made us look somewhat comical. And we flailed at each other under the stern direction of Coach Ball. Maybe 25 or so of us in total—not a big school. The 11 starters basically played both offense and defense. We eighth-graders served as the opposite "scout team" during the week for the starters to practice against. This was when I first played center. Not sure exactly how it happened—maybe there was no one else to do it and I volunteered, as I was apt to do. And on defense I still played defensive line.

Coach Ball, of course, had his own version of bull in the ring. Only he didn't fool around with padded blocking dummies. He constructed a small cage made of plastic PVC pipe set up low to the ground. Two players would square off inside the cage, and on the signal would try to drive the other one out. Coach Ball would be yelling "Butts down! Butts down! Drive! Drive! Drive!" as we fought each other for a few seconds. Then the next pair would go in. There was no hiding in this drill.

As an eighth-grader, I spent most of the season watching the ninth-graders play. And we (they) were good—so good that our SMJH team that year, in 1971, went 8-0 and won the Chattanooga junior high championship. For home games the stands were full—maybe a couple hundred people, Friday nights, under the lights. For away games we dressed in our old cinder block locker room that had a couple of old rusty weights off in a corner (no one lifted weights) and would ride the bus in uniform to our opponent's field in an old yellow school bus. We were tough, mean, and beat our opponents physically. Coach Ball-style. Not a lot of finesse.

At school, in contrast to Baylor, I found another world. No more uniforms (a relief), no more marching, no military men watching my every move. And girls were back in the equation, which, in eighth grade, actually had a bit more meaning than the old elementary school days. Oh, and classes were easy—so easy I got straight As with little effort. I usually had my homework done by the time I got home after the 45-minute bus ride home, or during study periods. Because I was one of the few kids actually "studying" in study period, I found time to tutor other students to help them out, made friends, even got involved in the student government. When football was over, I tried basketball but realized my lack of height and any other basic basketball skills meant those days were over. Not much room on the court for a chunky kid with zero vertical leap.

Looking back on grades eight and nine, it is very strange to think I was doing really nothing athletically outside of football season, other than pickup basketball and touch football and generally running around as a kid with a lot of energy. I went to Signal Mountain Junior High because we lived on Signal Mountain, or really halfway up Signal Mountain. We lived off the main road about a mile on a roughly paved road, literally on the side of the mountain.

My dad designed and helped build our A-frame-type house, with views over the Tennessee River valley. We moved in when I was about 8, I think. And living on the side of the mountain, with my dad, meant plenty of physical labor was available. Needed a wall? My dad and, eventually I, would be making walls with old railroad ties. Concrete sidewalk? Get the cement, gravel, sand, water, mix it, and pour it ourselves. Cold winter nights? Plenty of trees around our property to cut down, cut up, and use for firewood. My dad was hell with a chainsaw, and he could go all day with that thing. The result would be one or two former trees, neatly sawed into 2-foot logs, hauled and stacked by our house, covered with sap, sawdust, and sweat. Then, part of my daily chores would be the splitting of the logs with a sledgehammer and iron wedge into quarters or eighths. Start the wedge with a tap, get it going, then full swings with the sledge. When I got older and better, I used an ax, which could be easier but required more skill to hit the grain and avoid injury. Split the wood, then haul it up to the back door for the fireplace.

When our "local" supply of trees ran low—no worries. My dad hauled the chainsaw equipment, and me, down the side of the mountain on our property where there were plenty of good trees for firewood. Another full day's work, another stack of logs, but at the base of a slope about 100 feet long and probably 30 degrees of slope. My dad's brilliant idea—pay me a nickel for every log I manhandled up the mountainside to our house. A frickin' nickel. Yes, 20 trips (could only do one 20-pound log or so at a time) climbing up a slippery dirt trail with an unwieldy log grasped in my arms, grunting, scrambling up to the house . . . 20 times for a buck.

This was part of the routine at our house for many years—part of growing up a Moore. Pretty unusual for the son of a lawyer to get exposed to this kind of pure brute work. When I watch some of the "modern" training methods used by athletes today—flipping big tires down a field, stair climbing and jumping with resistance, cross-training—hey, I was doing some of that stuff on the side of Signal Mountain when I was just a kid.

In ninth grade at a junior high school, of course, ninth-graders are kings (and queens) of the school. Even for me, a relative newcomer, I was one of the kings. Having done my time as an eighth-grade serf, I was now starting center and defensive tackle for the football team. And as I said, football was king of all sports. Coach Ball had some good returning players, and we once again started out strong. We ran our unbeaten streak to 5-0 and were convinced that we would duplicate the previous season's perfect record. We certainly believed that as we got on the school bus to travel across town to play East Ridge Junior High. But early on, things did not go our way. Miscues, fumbles, players making stupid mistakes. We lost the game, something like 13-7, climbed back on the bus, and sat silently for the long ride back. At some point later on, I heard that some of our key players had been drinking before the game. Yes, ninth-graders! That explained some of the problems we were having, but to me, it was inexcusable: they let down the team, and nothing was more important than the team.

We regrouped and won our last two games of the year. I missed the last game with a sprained knee. We were playing Hixson Junior High, and I was in on defense and twisted my knee in the second half. Down on the field, never having really been injured before, I remember my dad jumping over the low fence around the field and coming *out on the field* to see how I was doing. I managed to limp off, but the next week had to watch my eighth-grade understudy finish the season in my spot. We won and were co-champions of the league with our one loss. I was recognized with all-county honors as a center, and that pretty much set the course going forward for me in football. I was a center.

I would say ninth grade at SMJH was a happy year for me. I kind of had a girlfriend most of the year and was accepted by my peers as one of them. I even ran for and was elected class president, complete with dorky campaign posters ("Vote for Blake—He's No Snake in the Grass") and a speech to the entire student body. In that speech, I thanked them for letting me become part of their school, their friends, and pledged to repay them with hard work if elected. It worked, and I did.

No ninth-grade boy can have a ninth-grade year without complications. For me, I became very self-conscious about my body. I was still boyish, chunky—and I convinced myself that I needed to lose weight (after football season, of course). Many of my friends were maturing and "growing up"—hitting puberty. Not me. I went on a diet, a ninth-grade boy eating a bowl of salad for lunch. Weird. And ineffective, as the diet was *only* at lunch. I didn't lose any weight.

I also had my first, and really only, fight. Standard attire for ninth-grade "jocks" at SMJH was jeans and boots—like cowboy boots, but not fancy cowboy boots. I learned how to dress, and that became my standard attire too. In phys ed class one day, somehow I got into an escalating argument with one of the rougher kids in school. He was a football player too, so a teammate, but the season was over. He was one of those kids who looked about 5 years older than a ninth-grader (shaving!) and rode his motorcycle to school. One thing led to another, and at some point he spit on my boot, a big juicy quid. The trigger in my head went off (bull in the ring!). I went after him with a wild lunge, and fists flew for a few seconds. Ineffective fists, but enough to catch Coach Ball's attention when he walked into our class. Damn! Both of us were awarded 5 licks each with the "holy" paddle, of course administered in front of all our classmates.

Ninth grade went by fast. Classes and grades were easy. I was not really challenged academically, and my mom and dad noticed this, my mom especially. I think, but don't know, that there were some rather heated discussions between my parents about the original decision to leave Baylor and its academic excellence. At some point another decision was made. After ninth grade, I would be given the option to go *back* to Baylor.

Now, I had just spent two years getting used to a completely different school and social environment. Public school, kids from *every* economic condition, smart kids, average kids, motivated and unmotivated. And girls. I had figured out not just how to fit in, but how to thrive. These were my friends. *Now*, I was given the *choice* to leave my friends and go back to Baylor? Might seem an easy choice, but it wasn't. Most of my friends and teammates would be going to Red Bank High School, just at the foot of Signal Mountain. A few of my SMJH teammates, three or four, were also given the chance to go to Baylor. And Baylor had given up the military school (now it was just a full-fledged prep school—all boys, tie required), which, I am sure, made some difference to my dad. While given the choice, my mom made it clear where she thought I belonged. And to be honest, I don't remember if I agonized over the decision very much or not. But ultimately, the decision was made: I would go to high school at Baylor, and rejoin my old seventh-grade classmates once again in tenth grade.

High School (1973–1976)

NOW, OVER THE summer after my ninth-grade year to that tenth-grade August, a miracle (to me) occurred. I grew. From 5 foot 10 or so, I grew to 6 foot 3 and my baby fat seemed to dissolve away, stretched over the new body that had been delivered magically to me that summer. I was suddenly tall and, well, almost thin. Taller than my dad, taller than any relative of ours that we were aware of. So now, in a matter of months, I went from being a short, heavyset center, to one of the skinniest guys to ever play offensive line. But, given the lack of any natural skill or speed to play another position, I stuck with center. So when I arrived back at Baylor and Coach Fred Hubbs (a great name for a line coach!), our line coach, asked what position I played, there was only one answer: I play center.

He was skeptical.

As noted, high school football in the South, especially at Baylor, was religion. We reported in for practice in August, tenth-, eleventh-, twelfth-graders all together. We actually had training camp. Baylor was a combined day and boarding school, so we packed up and moved into the austere high school dorms for 2 weeks of football camp. Up for breakfast, stumble down the long hill to the locker rooms, and pull on our gear. From there, we were required to jog out to the practice fields down by the river, and at 9 in the morning it was already hot and humid. Two-hour practices in full pads, mainly spent getting pummeled by upperclassmen—as tenth-graders we were there primarily as blocking and tackling dummies. Lunch break. Rest. Back out to practice in the afternoon, when it was even hotter. More physical punishment. Jog back to the locker room, shower, hang up our sweaty gear to dry out for the next day (it never really did), dinner, some sort of team meeting, fall asleep after routine tenth-grade boys' misbehavior in the dorm, and get up and do it again. While it was a necessary part of playing football, I hated training camp and two-a-days. Of course, really, we all did. But training camp was where the soft got hard, the weak got strong, the nice got mean—or you chose another sport. Training camp, from tenth grade until I retired, was an exercise in survival, mental and physical.

At Baylor, football was the sport. In an all-boys school, if you were an athlete—or half an athlete—you played football. It was a "no-cut" team, meaning everyone could go out for the team, and everyone dressed for games. In any given year, there were 75–100 players out for the team, and we would all practice, and all dress. You can imagine in such a system many kids didn't play, especially for the mighty Baylor Red Raiders. We were expected to be good, and we were. We had so many good players that for the first time in my football experience, players usually only played offense *or* defense. Not both. We were becoming specialized.

Now, as a tenth-grader at age 15, mixing in with juniors and seniors who were 17 and even 18 years old, the physical differences were acute. I was still embarrassed to go in the group showers, tall, skinny, and almost hairless, with many guys who were practically men. On the field that meant many mismatches, and you had to learn fast or get run over. I was basically the scout team center, meaning I and 10 other tenth-graders would line up every day against our first-team defense and run plays. I would be using everything I had to block our junior or senior nose tackle, who was a veteran and showed me that. Tough, but a good way to learn. Often my face mask would be knocked sideways, or my chinstrap would be shoved into my nose, or I'd just get pushed aside. Get up, try again . . .

I realized early on that I was playing not just for a good Baylor team, but a special team. We ran the wishbone option offense, which basically meant 90 percent run, think about passing the other 10 percent of the time, and then run anyway. It was a power and speed running attack, and we had the skilled players to run it. These were guys who would go on to play in big college programs on scholarships—Alabama, Tennessee, Auburn, North Carolina. NFL fans will know one name from that 1974 Baylor team—Charlie Hannah, who played at Alabama and many years in the NFL. (Younger brother of NFL Hall of Famer John Hannah, who graduated Baylor 1969. Oddly enough, I would cross paths with John many years later.)

A great team. Almost 100 players. What was I doing? I was holding down the *fifth-string* center spot. That's right—*fifth string*. That meant that four guys had to go down before I went in the game. Well, actually, as I learned later that year, *five* guys would have to go down. We were playing a team, perhaps Howard High, and out came the mighty Baylor Red Raiders. Undefeated. We quickly scored and kept on scoring. Our coaches started substituting liberally, one of the advantages of playing for a powerhouse team. Into the fourth quarter, up by about 40 points, Coach Hubbs came over to do the next center substitution—fifth string! Yes, I'm going to finally get into a varsity game! Instead, he turned to a senior lineman, and sent him in ahead of me due to his senior status. Now, think about that for a minute. A senior—he was *fifth* string. He had endured training camps, practices, standing on the sidelines, for *3 years* to get his brief shot. So, I couldn't resent that he got to go in first, and as it turned out, even I got to play a few snaps at the end of the game.

Most of my action came on Mondays, when the junior varsity team would play other schools. Yes, other schools too fielded enough players for us to actually have a 7 or 8 game JV season. We won them all, we tenth-graders (and a few juniors), and kept pace with the undefeated varsity. That is where I got my real experience, able to put to use the skills and toughness I was developing while working against our varsity. And I *loved playing*—the games, the competition, winning, beating the guy across from me, the team—I loved it. Made all the sweat and hard work worth it. I looked forward all week to the next game.

The varsity was having a special year. Undefeated, taking opponents apart. Sometimes the margin was so big I'd sneak in at the end of a game. We blew out our hated rival McCallie in the annual contest, so well-attended each year that my junior and senior years the games were played at the local college stadium. We swept through the season and entered the Tennessee state playoffs. Even these other top schools couldn't handle our team. We won our first two playoff games handily and advanced to the state championship game, to be played in Memphis, Tennessee.

I am pretty sure this was the second time I'd ever been on an airplane, the first being a trip with my younger brother Bob to visit my mom's parents in New York City in the early '70s. Two notable memories from that first trip: Bob got sick all over my mom on the plane, and at the Bronx Zoo an elephant sneezed all over me—elephant snot from head to toe. Quite the trip. Anyway, the Baylor Red Raiders were headed to Memphis to play in the Tennessee AAA state championship game. Even fifth-string centers got to go and dress for the game.

We chartered a flight and made the quick hop to Memphis. I don't recall spending the night—I think we literally flew in, played, and flew back. We played in the Liberty Bowl Stadium, the same place they used to play the old college Liberty Bowl game, seating for tens of thousands. It was a bitterly cold evening, under the lights, in December. We had our normal uniforms, maybe a pair of long underwear, and if you were lucky enough to get one, a large red and gray cape that you could drape over yourself to block the wind. Limited value.

I spent the entire game on the sideline with the other tenth-graders and many others as we watched the starters fight it out on the frozen field. After one offensive series failed, one of our running backs came off the field furious and hurled his helmet at the bench. Unfortunately, that was where I happened to be watching the game, and his frozen helmet hit my equally frozen shin so hard I thought I would cry. Hardest hit of the season, no question, magnified by the cold. I'll never forget that pain (Mike Shumaker!) and never forget that we won the game 6-0 for the state championship and, later, the "mythical" national championship (ranked #1 in the USA poll). It was a great day to be wearing the Baylor uniform, and I was never so happy as I was to take it off, get warm, and have the team meal (McDonald's takeout) on the way home. What a year for a tenth-grader!

The rest of the tenth-grade year was filled with academics and more academics. You see, in two years at Signal Mountain Junior High, where I had received a great education in the "real world" of real people, I had fallen almost a full year behind my classmates academically. So, rather than being able to immediately fall back in with the top classes, I had to work my way back to the top of the pack through study and hard work. Even though athletics, and especially football, were extremely important at Baylor, so too the academic side. Slackers were not tolerated—academic rigor was expected. And, of course, I had my mom there to make sure I never forgot that. If I came home with a 95 on a test, she would compliment me . . . and then ask if anyone had gotten a 100. If we had an assignment due in a week, she would suggest (daily) that I get started now and finish early. If I had done my math homework—had I checked my work? Twice? When we were required occasionally to turn in typed work, my mom would type the paper for me, but if I had a misspelled word in my paper, she would *type it misspelled* (that had to make her hands cramp up!). Her standard was to be the best, at everything, and she truly believed that I (and my two brothers) could be the best at anything I did. Anything. My drive to succeed, and to compete, and to be the best? Just check in with my mom.

My dad, on the other hand, was about hard work, discipline, not taking the easy way. We didn't hire out when we needed to build a new deck, or pour concrete, or mow the lawn, or haul wood up the side of the mountain. When I got a summer job working for a veterinarian on the top of Signal Mountain (which I held for several years), I wasn't dropped off at work during the summer. I rode my 10-speed Schwinn bike over 2 miles *up* the mountain highway, traffic whizzing by, no helmet (in those days), and got to work by 7 or 7:30 in the morning. Call it part of my summer training regimen. Of course, the ride home was great!

The non-football season at Baylor (winter and *part* of spring) entailed deciding what other athletic activity to participate in. Unfortunately, I had given up basketball when still a short, heavy eighth-grader, before my recent growth spurt. And at Baylor, doing something athletic after class was *required*, not optional. So, I could participate in some organized varsity sport or sign up for the much-ridiculed "GA," or "general athletics," as it was known. Today, it would stand for geek athletics—it was an after-school activity program for those who had little athletic skill or desire, but had to satisfy the requirement. Those of us who played football *never*, on principle, would sign up for GA. So I signed up for wrestling, under Coach Major Worsham, in the winter season. One of the hardest, scariest three months I ever spent in a sport.

Every day, we would troop into an overheated sauna of a wrestling room reeking of sweat, puke, and hormones from 50 adolescent boys. Coach Worsham put us through some of the most grueling 90-minute workouts I've ever been through, all the while punctuated by his shrill marine drill-sergeant voice screaming, "You gotta be mean! You gotta be mean!" Hand-to-hand combat. His favorite "terminal move" was to get a headlock on your opponent and grind his face up into your sweaty armpit, where upon Coach Worsham would be yelling, "Soak it! Soak it!" to basically encourage you to smother your opponent into submission.

There I was, all 6 foot 3, 170 pounds of beanpole, wrestling at my weight. Everyone else was *losing* weight to "wrestle down" at a lighter weight class. Not me. I think I was the only wrestler for Coach Worsham who actually gained weight, against all odds, during wrestling season. The growth spurt had kicked in, and it wouldn't be denied. I ate, I grew, and I learned to get tough under Coach Worsham's fierce glare. Surrender was simply not an option. My wrestling stint only lasted the one season, with a few junior varsity matches. But it was enough to leave a lasting impression on me: find another winter sport!

Springtime was track season, which, for most of us lineman, meant another season with Coach Worsham. Yeah, he coached track too. For the football guys it was really a long conditioning drill . . . unless you were Charlie Hannah and threw the shot put or discus, while the rest of us scraggly kids watched him in awe. And then somewhere in the middle of the spring, lo and behold, we varsity football players would all leave the track team and go suit up for spring practice. Yes, spring practice—full pads, full contact, full scrimmages for two weeks. This was like a Division I college program!

Now, I should add here that at this time, 1973–1974, there was still very little weight lifting going on. It just was not part of the regular training program. Running, calisthenics, a lot of push-ups. But little if any organized weight lifting. There were weights and bars in a dark old room off the gym at Baylor, but it was usually empty. I had a classic old set of Sears-type weights at home, probably totaled 100 pounds, seldom used. And there was really little instruction from our coaches on lifting weights, or how/when to do it. But at some point in my tenth-grade year, I began to wander into the weight room and do some lifting and watch what a few of the other senior football players were doing. These were guys who were going on to play big-time football at schools like Tennessee and Alabama, so I figured they must know what they were doing. And to me, still a skinny kid in the middle of growing up, they looked like *men* to me. I wanted to be strong too, I wanted to grow up, and so I started lifting weights on my own and copying what they did. Nothing extensive, but a start. And in the summertime, while working at the vet clinic, in addition to my bike ride up the mountain every day, I added a ride out to old Signal Mountain Junior High where I would run on my lunch hour, do some push-ups and sit-ups, and ride back to work. This in the hot

Chattanooga summer. I was learning the discipline it would take for me to realize my ambition, which was to not just be on the Baylor football team, but be a *starter* on the football team. I learned that getting in shape meant working hard every day, not just when I felt like it. I learned how to push myself, even though there was no Major Worsham yelling at me over the summer. But I knew what I wanted and figured hard work would get it for me. I never really questioned whether I would succeed—I just knew what I had to do.

In the meantime, I was eating my parents out of house and home, constantly feeding my growing body. About the only thing they could afford to give me in large quantities that was really healthy was milk, which became my staple food. And a lot of it. It was cheaper than soda, and it was served with breakfast, lunch, and dinner. I should have done commercials.

Rolling out of that summer of '74 into August training camp, I had put on some weight and muscle, and added confidence. At 6 foot 4, 180 pounds, I certainly wasn't intimidating as a center, but what I lacked in size I made up for in determination and smarts. Back to the dorms for two weeks of hellish practice by the Tennessee River, but this time with some understanding of the offense and offensive line play at the high school level. I was set to leave fifth string far behind me and got some playing time on the varsity. Charlie Hannah (many seasons as an NFL lineman) had graduated from the national championship team, but his brother David was an anchor at right tackle, and the Baylor Red Raiders were set to run through another strong season. Several of my junior classmates were moving up to start on the varsity, because we had a very talented junior class. Remember, many of these guys I had been playing with since fourth grade, and together we had lost only a couple of football games over all those years. These guys were good and knew it.

As things sorted out during preseason camp, it looked like I would be backing up a senior at center. We sweated and ran our way through the August months, right up to our preseason "jamboree" where 10 or 12 high school teams gathered at one field on a late-summer Friday or

Saturday night to play a series of one quarter "scrimmages" under the lights. A sort of live "tune-up" before our first game. First- and second-stringers would usually get a little playing time. And right about here, my junior season took an interesting turn—the senior center broke his arm. Just like that, I was the varsity starting center for the team expected to, once again, challenge for the state championship. And as a junior, I was playing alongside mainly seniors with a few junior superstars sprinkled in. I was no "superstar," but I did love the fact that I got to start and play every game. How great was this! And the senior center was going to be back in a few weeks from his injury so I was determined to make the most of my opportunity. I not only survived my first nervous start, but played pretty well, and we won the first few games. Coach Hubbs would yell at me during game film sessions to never turn sideways during a game, or he couldn't see me on film—too skinny! Ha-ha. But I was playing center for the mighty Red Raiders! The senior did eventually come back, but I was playing well and rather than bench me, Coach Hubbs let us split time, which was fine with me.

Another skill I learned early on as a center should be explained here: long snapping. On every punt and every field goal and every extra point, the center has to snap the ball back to the punter, for a punt, or the holder, for a kick. About 12–13 yards for a punt, exactly 7 yards for a kick. The centers in those days, and throughout my career, did this by looking back through their legs, snapping the ball back with two hands in a tight spiral (hopefully), to a very specific target area. A little off, and the punt or kick could be blocked. But, as you might imagine, this was not a skill very many football players had, or wanted to have. First, it was hard to do well. It took extra practice time and had little upside (a good snap was "expected") but tremendous downside (a bad snap could change an entire game). Second, it was usually painful: snapping the ball between your legs, with your head looking back at the target, left you very vulnerable to getting pounded by the defensive lineman. And it was not only acceptable, but coached by some, to literally knock the center silly on every long snap, in the hope that eventually the abuse would cause one bad snap. It took not only skill, but steel nerves, to line up and long-snap as a center.

In any event, beginning I believe in junior high school, at good old SMJH, the starting center was *expected* to also handle all the long-snapping duties. It was simply part of being a center. There were no specialists to run on for one play to snap the ball on kicks—not at SMJH and not in high school. I had heard there were specialists like that at big universities where they had 100 good players. But where I played, the center handled the regular center duties (snap to the quarterback, calling line assignments, blocking) and also the long-snapping responsibilities. This skill would prove to be quite meaning-ful in a few years. And I learned to handle it as part of my repertoire.

Our fall season '74 was a good one, but we were following on the heels of the best team in Baylor history. Expectations were high and continued to grow as we beat McCallie in the annual grudge match and cruised through the regular season undefeated, with a bruising running attack and a quarterback who actually was allowed to throw the ball downfield occasionally. The McCallie game was a memo-rable one for me. We were tied just before halftime 7-7. We were forced to punt, and I was the center and, hence, the long-snapper. We executed the punt and covered the returner well downfield. Penalty. Our *punter* (and also our senior QB) had failed to put his mouthpiece in on the play. What?! Fifteen-yard penalty, re-kick. We were play-ing in front of several thousand fans (that's right, a *high school* foot-ball game) under the lights at the local college stadium. I remember I thought it was strange they actually painted the grass to make it greener—it came off on our pants. We lined up to redo the punt—and I snapped the ball a good three yards over the hands of our leaping punter. The ball carried clear back into the end zone where McCallie recovered it for a touchdown, and the halftime lead, 14-7. I was hor-rified. Embarrassed. I had just done that in front of the biggest crowd I had ever played before. I had let my team down and went into the locker room bitterly disappointed. We regrouped, my team supported me, and we came out and scored several touchdowns in the second half to blow away McCallie and erase my mistake from the first half, but *never* from my memory. And I used that memory to drive myself to be better.

We ended the regular season undefeated, which sent us into the state playoffs again. Of course, playoffs meant practicing into late November. This November of 1974 the team gathered early Thanksgiving morning, Thursday, to get a cold practice in before we were dismissed to eat our turkey and pie. I am sure there were some parents not too happy about that schedule. In fact, it interrupted our traditional Thanksgiving breakfast at church, which couldn't have made my dad very happy. He would have argued church and family first, football second. But my parents were balanced, because my mom would have argued the opposite—football first! Anyway, practice we did. But our bid for a second straight championship fell short as we lost in the first round of the playoffs, to our archrival, McCallie, a disappointing end to the season, but a great season for me personally because I started and played so much as a junior.

Through all this football, the rigorous academic schedule continued. I had studied my way almost back to par with my classmates from the academic progress lost while in junior high school. I was taking some advanced placement, or "AP," courses that would eventually give me college credit if I scored well enough. Though the military was gone, the tough teachers were *not*. Competition for grades was fierce. Teachers had many bright students and few average ones. Poor students washed out quickly. Teachers were all male, with one or two exceptions. My literature/writing teacher one year was a skinny, curly-haired hyperactive guy who often taught while walking around the classroom, between our chairs, and on top of his desk. He would grade essays fiercely—*any* misspelled word, typo or not, was minus 5 points. Three misspelled words in an essay and the *best* grade you could get was a B (85), and that was *before* he ripped into grammar and content. Getting an A in his class was an accomplishment.

We had some choices in our classes, mainly in language,

literature, and history. But math and science were a hard-core part of the curriculum, and the top students fought for the top classes and top grades. We could get some impossible assignments. Our physics teacher senior year handed out one such assignment. I have mentioned Baylor sits along the Tennessee River, with water levels significantly controlled by TVA constructed dams. Part of the Baylor campus included a lake of sorts, but it was really a giant mudflat that rose and fell depending on the river's level. In essence, it was a big polluted overflow puddle, big enough for canoeing and old tires and other junk, and not much else. Maybe 2–5 feet deep and probably 10 feet of mud.

Well, our physics teacher wanted the class to calculate the volume of water in that "lake," using all kinds of mathematical formulas, depth readings taken by canoe, and contour maps. We teamed up with one other person in class for the project (looking back, I think that was for safety purposes in case someone fell in). I teamed up with the smartest guy in the class, and a good friend, Maury Levine.

After many hours on the water in a canoe, with formulas and calculators and maps and no answer, we one day looked at each other and came to a solution: call the TVA—this was their damn lake, and they had to know what the volume was! Brilliant! Of course, they knew. When we turned in our results, our professor was both miffed and pleased. Miffed because we took a shortcut; pleased because we used a unique solution methodology that was "in bounds"—he hadn't placed any restrictions on getting the answer—just *get* the answer. That "A" felt good. Our classmates were impressed (or pissed off).

Winter of my junior year I decided to move out of the sweaty wrestling room and into a sport I had never tried before: soccer. Now, bear in mind this was 1974. There were few, if any, "kids' soccer leagues," especially in Chattanooga, Tennessee. In fact, most high schools didn't even *have* a soccer team. There was no such thing as a "soccer mom." But it had to be better than wrestling, and I had, unfortunately, given up on basketball too soon (when still short and fat!).

All I knew about it was the general concept of running a lot (which I figured would help keep me in shape for football—remember, all other sports were training for the *real* sport), a round ball, and no hands. Oh, and there seemed to be some opportunity for physical contact at some positions. So I tried out for the varsity team. In Tennessee, as a winter sport, we trained and played in shorts no matter the temperature. And trust me, it can be cold and wet in Chattanooga in January.

I trained hard, ran hard, and learned some of the basic ball handling skills so that I was a passable player (for that day and age—*never* today!). But what I really brought to the field, and which won me a starting spot as defensive fullback, was my football/lineman mentality. I looked for contact, I tried to collide with the opponents with the ball near our goal. I was perhaps the biggest guy on the field *whenever* we played, and those little quick offensive soccer players weren't so quick when I was running right at them, hoping to touch the ball so I had an excuse to run them over. It was crude, but effective. We didn't give up many goals, and actually went all the way to the state finals and won the championship, the state high school championship! Now, granted, there were probably only about 15 high schools in the whole state that fielded a soccer team at the time, but we won the championship. To be able to go out and play a sport I had never tried before—and *win*—it was great fun. I knew I'd be playing again senior year.

Springtime, oh, beautiful springtime in Tennessee—well, that meant more football practice, with some track meets wrapped around spring ball. Full pads, full contact, either earning or cementing a starting spot for the next fall season. In track, this spring, Major Worsham thought it would be a good idea for me—tall, lanky me—to learn to run the high hurdles in addition to throwing the discus. The high hurdles turned out to be not such a good idea. I ended up running *through* more hurdles than I ran over, and after a week or so strained my back. Just not built to run. But throwing the discus, and running to stay in shape, and getting into the weight room for some lifting, all proved to be good spring training for football.

That summer, I kept my job at the vet clinic on top of the mountain, which included my rides up the mountain each morning. As well, I kept up my routine of riding my bike a couple miles to SMJH at noon, and running a mile or so in the hot sun, and biking back to work. Weight lifting was still sporadic—more push-ups and sit-ups than anything else. There were no fitness centers around in those days, at least not near where we lived on the side of Signal Mountain. This was also the first year that I "opted out" of our family vacation, traditionally a week or two at the beach in South Carolina (Pawleys Island). I didn't want to miss work or workouts that close to football season. Plus, with a girlfriend, and a car available to me, hanging out at home wasn't so bad anyway. Not that I did much more than work, workout, and go out on dates, anyway. But being my own "man" for a while was good. My parents reluctantly agreed, though they, especially my dad, questioned my priorities (working out for the football team??). But it was important to me, and I insisted.

My life in high school was very structured and disciplined. During the school year, my dad would take us to school at around 7:15 in the morning, and I'd get picked up after sports at around 5 or 5:30 in the afternoon, 5 days a week.

Saturdays were for recovering from Friday sports activities and doing homework. Sundays—*every* Sunday, was church all morning, and usually back to church for Sunday evening youth group or other church-related activities. I might get out on a date with my girlfriend on Friday (unless there was a football game) or Saturday. During vacations, both summer and other breaks, I normally worked days at the veterinary clinic, 8-hour days. During junior and senior years, I also was the after-hours janitor there—I'd drive up after practice, clean the building (sinks, floors, tables, baseboards) for an hour and a half, drive home, finish homework, go to bed. I liked the money, and my mom loved that I was so busy. I think I liked it too—I was never one to be able to just lay around for very long. In part, because I was so busy, in part, because I changed schools and friend sets, and in part, because both my mom and dad embedded a deep sense of right and wrong in me, I never really became part of the teenage party scene in the '70s. I'm sure it was going on, but I was too busy to get involved in the parties. Other than an occasional sip of cold beer at home with my dad at the end of a long day of chainsawing, I never really liked or drank beer (or alcohol) until I got to college. Some would say I was sheltered. I'd say I was just too busy trying to excel and succeed to bother with it.

For me, those two words were the key: *excel* and *succeed*. Whether I was born with the gene, or my mom (!!) and dad drilled it into me, or both—I wanted to excel and succeed in whatever I did. School—if I didn't get all "As" I was upset—it drove me to work harder. I don't think I got a "B" until I was in college (and that caused me to change my major! Well, sort of . . .). As I mentioned, I was in fierce competition with Janet Zuckerman all through elementary school—to see who had the best grades. Same at Baylor—I wanted to be the top in the class. Extra credit assignments? I did them all. Bonus points? Sign me up. Grades were a measuring stick of my success, and I wanted to be the best.

Sports too were another opportunity to excel and succeed. The drive to be the best made me one of the most competitive kids around. I always wanted to win—whether against my peers, the other team, the defensive lineman across from me—I just wanted to win. My middle brother, 5 years younger than I was—I still wanted to beat him—whether a board game or pickup basketball. Wrestling, basketball, tennis, racquetball, football, pickup games, church league, junior varsity, high school—I had an intense desire to compete and to win. And I *always* thought I should, and could, win. If I didn't, it wasn't because the other person was actually better than I, but rather because I had failed—to work hard enough, try hard enough, prepare hard enough, whatever. I thought I could—and should—win. I thought I could—and should—excel and succeed. And I had a core belief that if I worked hard enough, I *could do anything* I wanted to. And, looking back, "success" in school and sports was largely the way I validated myself to my parents, my peers, and myself. It made me feel accepted and valuable, and in a way, that was intoxicating. Once successful, I wanted more.

Senior year in high school was set up to be a gem. After a long hot summer of working out, I felt fully ready to be the starting center for the Baylor Red Raiders. And we figured to have a good team, really good. Several of our senior starters were already "set" to go to large universities to play football. Our starting fullback could run over you or away from you—pick your poison. Our quarterback was not only a good runner but very good at running the triple option from our wishbone formation. He too could keep the ball and go the distance, or pitch it to one of our other backs to sweep around the end. Our offensive line was solid, and we knew our assignments well. No more Hannah brothers (the youngest, David, had graduated last year—I'm not sure I ever saw him smile on the football field—he was too busy grinding the opponent into the ground). Since I was a returning starter, and the center, I was expected to be one of our top offensive lineman and leader of the team. I came in at about 6 foot 5, 200 pounds now, and still growing. I was confident, as was the rest of the team, as we worked and sweated through two-a-day practices in the thick Chattanooga August air. Once we started our season, we felt no one could—or should—beat us, and we played that way. Our ground game averaged over 300 yards per game. We scored over and over, and the second- and third-string players got to play quite a bit. In one game, we scored a touchdown every time we had the ball in the first half. It was 35-0 at halftime. Our coach told the starters we were done for the evening—that we were to watch the halftime show (the opposing school had a terrific band!), get showered, and head home *before the game was over*. One of the strangest games ever, but a testament to how good we were. Our success continued, and we rolled through the regular season undefeated, 10-0, including a shellacking of McCallie played under the lights before thousands at the University of Tennessee—Chattanooga stadium.

In the first round of the playoffs we were on the road against a team who had one of the best middle linebackers in Tennessee high school history. In fact, I think he had already signed to go play for the University of Tennessee. As the center, on most running plays the middle linebacker was my responsibility. I would fire off the line and try to get to him (he was 3 yards off the line) and block him before he could get to our running back. He was so fast, it was almost impossible to get to him to get a block. And when I did it was like hitting a stone wall. This guy was 6 foot 4, 225 pounds of grown man, and when he hit me with his forearm under the chin, I knew it. It was one of the first times I had played against someone who was simply better than I was, physically. Faster, stronger, quicker. I was determined, but not very effective. Neither was the rest of our team, as we lost to McMinn County, 14-7 on that cold November night. Playoffs over. Senior season over. Just like that.

I was shocked. We were all shocked. It was the first time I really had to contemplate whether I would ever play organized football again. My life for years had been one football season rolling into another, every year, as inevitably as I grew up. Now, with the final whistle, high school football was over. I had been recruited lightly (some letters) to play football at some of the big universities. It was fun to get a letter from the University of Tennessee or Auburn, asking if I would be interested in playing football at their fine schools. But I had already made up my mind that I wanted to go to a small school for college, a liberal arts college. I hadn't really spent a lot of time figuring out where, or even if I would be able to play football wherever I did end up going. So for me, this unexpected loss was sudden and disconcerting. No more football?

I collected some very nice all-city and all-county first-team center awards, and, most meaningful to me, the Most Valuable Offensive Lineman Award for our Baylor team. This award was given by Coach Hubbs, who I had come to admire and respect over the years for his coaching skills, but also his patience with a skinny, slow but determined tenth-grader who eventually put on enough weight to be seen on film doing a good job—even when he turned sideways. I was honored to even be in the same category of honoree as the Hannah brothers had all been. Very special to me.

Of course, one of the benefits of being a good high school athlete is that as soon as one season ends (even in disappointment), another begins. Winter meant soccer time, and we were the defending state champs. Granted, state champs in Tennessee, but champs nevertheless. We took the field with confidence—the cold, sometimes muddy, field—most of our starters returning. In one January game, I remember it was frigid—and, of course, we were in soccer shorts. I made my usual aggressive defensive move on the ball/opponent (was there a difference?), but this time his knee caught me flush in my thigh. Almost brought tears to my eyes. It was one of the most painful injuries I had ever had. Waves of pain through the cold and numbness. I had trouble pushing off my leg. Come out of the game? No way. Part of the football mentality cultivated over years was to fight through the pain—you stayed on the field to play with your team unless you simply couldn't go. The deep thigh bruise nagged me for a couple weeks, but I didn't miss a practice or a game. We ended up in the state finals again, the championship game, and this time had to win it in an overtime "kickoff." Joy and excitement to have won it again, even in a "minor" sport like soccer.

About this time in my life, and I can't recall exactly when, though I am pretty sure it was after football season senior year, my life turned upside-down. Now, it is entirely possible that I was a naive kid—smart sure, but possibly naive. I had had a stable, textbook family for my entire life. Father a respected attorney. Stay-at-home mom whose primary mission was to be sure her sons were well-taken care of and had every opportunity to succeed (translation: we should be the best). I had been in exclusive private schools with a pretty select group of peers for all my life, with the exception of my 2-year public school "sabbatical." We went to church every Sunday, usually twice, family church camp every summer. I just didn't see anything coming. But it did come—my parents got separated. Their marriage was not working. My dad left the house, moving out. Explanations were made, but didn't really register or make any sense to me. Sure, I was 17 years old at the time, and I knew people got divorced, and men and women fell out of love. But not *my* parents, not *my* father, not *my* mother, not in *my* world. Things, I guess, were a lot more complicated than they seemed.

How did I respond? I took refuge in the things I did well. I doubled down on my studies, my athletics, my work. I felt that the only person I could count on, absolutely, was myself. And I was not going to let myself down. So as my parents were separated, getting counseling, reconciling, crying, fighting (never physical), re-separating—all during my senior year of high school—I focused all my attention and energy on excelling and succeeding in the things I believed I controlled: school, athletics, work. I did my best to ignore, emotionally and otherwise, what was going on in my family. I remember one time when things got heated between my parents, and I was there, I simply walked out of the house, up our driveway, and sat down on a rock. My rock. My place away from the emotional mess. My mom pleaded for me to come in, she cried for me to come in, but I sat stoically there on my rock, impervious externally, emotionally wrecked internally. But I refused to let any of this get in the way of the things I felt I could control. It was my way of fighting back against the things going on in my life that I couldn't control.

I've never written any of this down before. Talked about it with only a few people. Hard stuff. And I'm sure I haven't figured out all the implications. But I was bound and determined not to let what was going on at home impact my life outside of home. I continued to excel at school and at sports. Spring of my senior year at Baylor I was on the track team, but really it was just a little discus practice, and then working out and lifting weights. I had channeled more of my emotional energy into getting bigger and stronger. I also was going through the process of deciding which college to go to.

College selection in early 1976 was very different than college selection these days (and I went through it with my two kids in the early 2000s, so I *know*). No visits, road trips, weekends with students, Webcams, or photo tours. I knew I wanted (or thought I knew—I think it was one of those thoughts implanted by my dad at an early age) to go to a very high-quality small liberal arts college. Not one of the big universities that many of my friends were going to. And how to choose? No real college counseling program at Baylor. You took the SATs, got your scores, and then looked at the schools you *might* qualify for. With my grades and SATs, I probably could have made a go at an Ivy League school, but those also seemed large and intimidating to me. I definitely wanted to go *away* to college (*away* from the family dynamics), so I almost randomly explored three colleges: Colby (Maine), Carleton (Minnesota), and Wooster (Ohio). The first two were on size, location, and academic merit alone. Wooster, on the other hand, was part of our family history. My dad, his dad, and *his* dad (my great-grandfather) had all gone to Wooster. I gathered all the information I could (I think it entailed a color catalog from each college), and the application materials. Colby and Carleton required essays to apply. Wooster did not. I chose Wooster. And I was pretty confident they'd let me in, which they did. Interestingly, football in college for me was really a secondary consideration. First, I wanted a school where I'd get a good education, and second, I'd think about football. That is what led me along the way to send back notes to the large football programs thanking them for their interest but letting them know I would be going to a small college. And Wooster it was.

I was never "recruited" by Wooster. No calls by a football coach there, no letters, no offers for a visit. Once I was accepted, I got a letter in the mail from the Wooster football coach. Inside was a postcard, postage prepaid. The postcard asked me to answer a simple question: "Do you plan to play Wooster Fighting Scot football?" There was a yes box and a no box. I checked yes, with little thought other than, "of course," and sent the postcard in. Several years later, sitting and talking with my Wooster offensive line coach, he told me I was one of their "top recruits" that year. Really?! And that pretty much summed up recruiting for college football at a Division III, no scholarships, small college in 1976.

With that decision made, senior year played on out. I was

immersed in school, and training, and trying to avoid dealing too much with my parents' separation. I have some recollection that they reconciled temporarily for my graduation, but that was never really going to work out. Trust, once broken, is almost impossible to fix. I collected some nice awards at graduation and gave the salutatorian speech to the entire assembly at graduation. Of course, this was the runner-up speech to the valedictorian, which my mom was having trouble understanding. How could I not be number one?! As it turned out, the valedictorian was my good friend, Maury Levine, who has remained a dear friend all my life, so I don't think I shed a tear over second place. But I didn't *play* for second place.

Ever.

Summer after my senior year is kind of a blur. I had taken a new summer job because I wanted to make more money ($5 an hour! vs. the minimum wage at the vet clinic), and it entailed doing manual labor in a flour mill 8 hours a day throughout the hot summer. Average temperature in the mill was around 85 at 7 a.m. when I punched my time clock, and more like 95 most of the day in an enclosed, non-airconditioned building. I was sweat-soaked by 7:15 a.m., and stayed that way all day until I punched out at 3:30 p.m. From there, I would drive to Baylor, run and lift weights, and then go home, exhausted. My social life involved church on Sundays and dates with my girl-friend. But she had gone off to college the year before so though we were still dating, there seemed much less purpose to it. My dad had an apartment somewhere, and I and my brothers were supposed to see him at least once a week. We made the most of it, awkwardly. It was a long, hot summer. Needless to say, there was no family vacation that year.

There was, however, some football in the summer of '76. Unexpectedly, I was invited to play in the Tennessee East-West All-Star Football game, a contrived event held every summer for graduated seniors who were going to play college ball. I have the impression I may have been a substitute, since almost everyone else invited was going to play for a big university. But I wasn't going to turn down the honor. The Easterners and Westerners gathered at Middle Tennessee State University for a week of practice. I got to play alongside a lot of future big college stars. I think, even with my added weight, that I was one of the lightest offensive linemen there (all 205 pounds of me). After a week of practice we played a spirited game. I remember we won the game, and I recall two other things. First, the MTSU coaches offered me a scholarship if I'd come play for them—a very nice compliment which I politely declined. Second, the West nose tackle punished me all night long. One of the toughest guys I'd ever played against directly on my nose all night. He gave me a dose of the intensity I would need to play at the college level, and it was a wake-up call. I hung in there, but it was a battle. High school was over.

It finally came time to pack up and head off to college. Though nervous about leaving, I could hardly wait to get away from the emotional drama that surrounded my family and restart my own life. Some of that is normal, ready-to-go-to-college stuff. But I know I was escaping too.

CHAPTER 4

The College of Wooster (1976-1980)

WE LOADED UP all my stuff to go to Wooster. Remember, I'd never even visited, or seen a picture of it other than in the college catalog. It was actually surprising how little I had to pack. My stereo equipment took up most of the space. The rest was mainly jeans, T-shirts, some tennis shoes, and "snow boots" (like I knew what those were—they were actually just my work boots), and some coats that I thought, or my mom thought, would keep me warm in the cold Ohio winter. Wooster, Ohio. Roughly 580 miles north of Chattanooga, through Kentucky, Cincinnati, and past Columbus, but 45 minutes short of Cleveland. Yeah, kind of the middle of nowhere, or at least it felt like it when my dad and I turned off Interstate 71 for the short state road into the town of Wooster. The yellow Ford Maverick ("3 on the tree" stick shift, clutch barely operable) was stuffed to the gills. My mom was more or less distraught when I left, but lucky for her she had my two younger brothers to focus her intense motherly love on. I was ready to go.

Mid-August 1976, about 2½ weeks before any of the other college kids would arrive. This felt a bit like when my mom dropped me off for the first time at Signal Mountain Junior High School. I had never been here before, had never met any of the other football players who were all checking in for camp. I had not been in touch with the coaches, other than the aforementioned intensive recruiting campaign. After our 10-hour drive up, we literally pulled in, found the coach checking players in, found my room assignment, and unloaded all my stuff and clothes into a tiny, unairconditioned dorm room that would be football camp home for 2½ weeks. I met my roommate, Mike Riffee, who would be my roommate for my first two years of college. He was a running back, Ohio native, short, strong, fast, and good-natured. We hit it off immediately. I shook my dad's hand good-bye, waved at the ol' Maverick, and turned forward to my new life.

Wooster was (is) a small liberal arts college, one of many like it in Ohio. NCAA Division III, so no scholarships. The football players here were playing because they loved the game and wanted to play at the college level but weren't big enough or fast enough to play for a university or big college. All were serious about playing (well, OK, most), and were here to compete and win.

Wooster had been through a tough few years of football—the prior four years the Fighting Scots were 10-23. Wooster has one of the oldest college football traditions in the United States. In fact, my great-grandfather, Robert Moore, played on the first Fighting Scot football team, the 1889 Scots who demolished Denison twice that year for a cumulative score of 98-0. The next year, Wooster took on Ohio State, looking for a little more competition, but waxed the Buckeyes 64-0. That is not a typo. Wooster played Ohio State a few more times the next several years, and apparently after the 1908 Wooster win, Ohio State had had enough. In the 1909 rematch, Ohio State rolled up its sleeves and its recruits and dominated with a 74-0 rout. But one of those old game balls, from a victorious Wooster vs. OSU contest had, and still has, a prominent place in the trophy case on campus. The last game of the series was played in 1925.

Plenty of history and tradition behind Wooster Fighting Scot football, and I and the rest of the eager young freshmen were excited to be a part of the program. Our class of freshmen was larger than in the past—we had probably 25 or so guys come out for the team, for a total team size of maybe 60. Already I noticed the difference from Baylor football, and Tennessee high school football: every able-bodied male did not automatically go out for the football team. In fact, many good athletes played other sports as their primary sport. *What?!* Unthinkable from where I came from.

Generally, the freshman class of players was the largest, and then talent, other interests, and sometimes injuries would whittle each progressing class down over the four years of playing. Our freshman class that started out so large and full of fight, was down to under 10 by our senior year.

But none of that mattered much to any of us when we showed up and checked out our practice gear for the first set of two-a-day practices. Gold nylon pants, white mesh practice jerseys (offense; defense wore black), and the usual complement of leg, hip, shoulder pads, and helmets. Helmet technology had advanced a bit, but very little by my first year of college—at least at Division III college. Still the old "bell-ringer" suspension strap helmets, with maybe a tad more padding than before. We dressed in a small, windowless spartan locker room made of concrete and steel lockers with space on top to throw your shoulder pads and helmet after practice to dry out.

For the first two weeks, the football team was pretty much the only students on campus. We started practicing earlier than all the other sports, so just us guys. All we had was practice, meals together, team meetings, and then home to the same dormitory (we all stayed together during camp—in this way very much like Baylor). We quickly got to know everyone on the team, and, of course, freshmen were the lowest rung of the ladder. We knew nothing, and as a result, got to do all the "extras" every practice: carry the blocking dummies out and back, balls, water coolers, other equipment. All part of paying our dues as freshmen.

I reported into camp in the best shape of my life, 6 foot 5, and 215 pounds. That made me one of the largest offensive linemen on the team. There were a couple others bigger, one of whom was the incumbent starting center, a senior. But when the coaches asked me my position, I said "center," not just "offensive line." They had me experiment with other positions on the line, but home was center, and my athletic and mental skills were suited for the position. We pounded away at each other during two-a-days for two weeks, and I was sore and tired for most of that time. I was getting practice time with the first line, as a freshman, which was a pretty big deal to me. I set my sights on starting, being the first-team center as a freshman. Once I made that my goal, I was determined to make it happen.

I picked up the offense quickly. The speed of the game, and talent of the players, I found similar to the better talent I had played against in Tennessee—there was just more consistently good talent in college, as one would expect even at the DIII level. I had a good offensive line coach, who was with me all four years of my college career—Art Marangi. He kept me on my toes, pushed me, and understood I could be much better. Ultimately, he made a decision that shook up the offensive line but showed me an amazing amount of confidence in a freshman: he moved the senior incumbent from center to tackle, and put me in as the starting center. I was nervous, excited, and confident, all at the same time, and I hadn't even been in my first college football game. That was coming soon. We had a live scrimmage with another small college, Grove City, toward the end of August, to test ourselves. We were ready, I was ready, to get the season started.

But before the season started, school started. College started. All new, all different. Sign up for classes, hope to get the ones you want. When I started college, given my experience at the veterinary clinic, I had some vague idea that I would be a vet or a doctor, so I signed up for science courses, all the intro level courses, which included afternoon 2–3-hour lab sessions once or twice a week. One of my first and best negotiations as a freshman was about my AP calculus credits. I had scored a 3 (out of 5) on the AP exam, at the end of high school. The Wooster registrar noted that the 3 score was right on the cusp of "no credit" for the AP exam, which would have been frustrating to me (I was getting one full credit each for history and English literature, where I scored 4 or better). But, the registrar went on, if I agreed not to take any math courses at Wooster (?!), they would give me *two* credits for my Calculus AP score and call it a day. Done deal,

I said. Wasn't headed down the math road, anyway.

I also had a freshman merit scholarship of $2,000 or so, applied against my tuition, and it entailed working with a biology professor who was doing some genetic research with fruit flies. My job, several afternoons a week? Anesthetize the little critters with ether, and then count them under a microscope by eye color or some other unique characteristic. The trick was to gas them enough to keep them still on the slide, get the count done, and then back in the tube before they started buzzing around. This highly skilled work went on for a semester, or until the project was over, or until I let too many of the flies escape . . . not exactly sure which.

As school began, we broke football camp, and we players separated off to our yearlong quarters and roommates. I stayed with Mike, and we hauled our meager belongings over to Kenarden Hall, a freshman dorm at the time, all men (no co-ed dorms at Wooster in 1976). Somewhat ironic, as my dad had spent some of his Wooster time in this very dorm as well. Perhaps *his* father too. The huge dorm was built in 1911, and was somewhat famous for being virtually indestructible—surviving multiple college classes, parties, winter storms, and even a fire. Mike and I moved in, tired from all the football practice but glad to get settled into our room. After a bit of rearranging, Mike ended up being more comfortable sleeping on the floor, *under* his bed, which, combined with certain culinary habits (2-gallon tub of peanut butter within ready reach), general disregard for "neatness", and his rather stocky stature, soon earned him the nickname of "Pig," which stuck throughout his college days and which his friends applied to him with great humor and warmth: it just fit, and rather than fight it, he embraced it.

As we got settled into first week of classes, it also meant our first game of the season, and my first college game. I really didn't know what to expect. At Baylor, we played in front of crowds ranging from several hundred to several thousand. The "stadium" at Wooster might hold, at capacity, about 4,000. No lights, with an all-weather track around it.

But my first college game was to be on the road, against Canisius College, a small college in upstate New York. *New York?* A drive of about 6 hours. We packed up our gear—and I mean we—each player—packed up our own gear. No equipment managers to do that for us—we had to make sure everything we needed was in the big black nylon travel bag: helmet, pads, jersey, pants, cleats, undershirt, jock, socks, mouth guard—any gear you wanted, you'd better pack it.

We assembled early Saturday morning for the bus ride to Canisius, a rare night game for us. The Wooster bus pulled up behind the phys ed center, ancient, black and gold school colors. It had approximately 250,000 miles on it, looked, and rode like it, and was irreverently referred to by most male athletic teams as the Fighting Scot Dildo. To accommodate the full football squad, down the center aisle of the bus, between each set of two seats on either side, was a fold-down piece of laminated plywood designed to serve as a jump seat for the freshmen who otherwise would have no place to sit. I took a look at this arrangement, flexed my starting status (even as a freshman) and large size, and scored a shotgun seat in the one team utility van that made the trip with the bus. *Six hours!*

On the way, we took a side trip that would eventually prove co-incidental. My line coach's brother was at the time a backup quarterback for the Buffalo Bills. He arranged for us to stop at the Bills' stadium for a tour of the facility and the Bills' locker room. Now, the most famous player in the NFL at the time was, in fact, playing for the Bills—O. J. Simpson, who was at perhaps the peak of his NFL career. I stopped in wonder in front of his locker, reached in, took out his helmet, and put it on. An NFL player's helmet—and not just any helmet. O. J.'s helmet. To this day, I remember one thing about that helmet—it was huge—it literally would spin around my head when I had it on. O.J. had one large head.

From the tour of an NFL stadium and facility, back on the Scot bus and van and on to Canisius. Well, not exactly Canisius. Turns out Canisius didn't have a home field, so we were playing at a local high school field, with a name something like Tyler and Palowadzinski

Field. I could hardly believe it when we pulled up—this was where my college football career would begin—a high school? Welcome to Division III football.

We piled out of the bus and van. It was cool and raining. I'm sure we got dressed in some cramped room under the bleachers, but really I can't remember. I do remember how excited I was to be starting my first college football game, and how anxious I was to do well, and how worried I was about screwing up a snap under the wet, muddy conditions we played in. And I was, of course, as the center, handling all the long-snapping responsibilities, something that could really be challenging in wet and muddy conditions. Somehow, we slogged our way to a 15-14 win. My highlights? I didn't mess up any snaps, and, in fact, while covering a punt, actually recovered a fumble by Canisius. We gratefully left with a win, showering up somewhere and climbing back on the bus/van for the 6-hour ride home after the game. No hotel overnight stay in the Fighting Scot football budget—drove straight to campus through the night and crawled into bed at some awful time in the morning—but at least at 1-0! And my first collegiate football game was under my belt.

As a college student, I really wasn't sure what to expect when classes started, and we were to show up and do academic work. Football—I knew what to expect—a tougher variation of what I'd been doing most of my life. I was pleasantly surprised to find that not only was I well-prepared (by Baylor) for the collegiate level academic rigors and approach, but that I enjoyed it, for the most part. While attending class in college was somewhat "optional," I never treated it that way, nor did I really want to miss classes. I showed up, I did the work, I was engaged in the class discussion. Like Baylor, there was an expectation that you would arrive in class prepared and involved. Now, that doesn't mean everyone did so, but generally I did. As noted, I thought I was "pre-med" at this time, so I was signed up for the entry level sciences courses—like chemistry. This included one or two laboratory sessions in the afternoons, 2–3 hours once or twice a week (*for no additional credit?!*), plus my freshman fruit-fly genocide project, so I was a very busy but happy camper my first few months of school. Especially when factoring in 2–3 hours of football per day, with games on Saturday. And for away games, that was basically the entire Saturday.

On the personal side, I was generally happy to be in college, with my new friends—and not at home dealing with the ruptured family. Now that's not to say I didn't get homesick. My mom lavished extraordinary love and attention on me and my brothers, making sure everything was "just right" for "her boys." And I missed my dog, Rocket, and "sort of" missed my girlfriend of a couple years. Sort of, because she had gone to college the year before, and I think we both could read the writing on the wall, so by the time I went off to college in the fall of '76, things had cooled down and at some point, I think with a lame and stilted letter from me, we decided to part as "friends" (who never really talked after that).

The party scene at Wooster was like the party scene at many small colleges in the '70s, I assume: every weekend, and with a wide variety and many involving disco music. The local fraternities (no national fraternities at Wooster) held their keggers every Saturday night, with loud rock 'n' roll and 3.2 beer. In Ohio, unlike my home state of Tennessee, the legal drinking age was 21, not 18. However, Ohio, in its infinite wisdom, decided that it would be OK for 18-year-olds to drink something called 3.2 beer, or "near beer," with about half the alcohol of normal beer. Of course, 18-year-olds found that to be a mere volume challenge.

There was the occasional local sorority-sponsored dance, or even a college-sponsored dance. Movies on campus and concerts were available if you wanted to do some dating, which I did very little of my first college semester. My roommate and best friend Pig had a similar social schedule, so we were quite compatible, and it would be a normal big Friday or Saturday night for us to go to the college campus movie, have some pizza delivered to our room, and be asleep by 11 or 12. Not big partiers.

Our second game of that year was also an away game, but this time against a similar Ohio small college, Kenyon, one of our conference opponents. Most of our games every 9-game season would be against other small Ohio liberal arts colleges very much like Wooster: 1,500–2,000 students, Division III, no scholarships, 50–75 players on the squad, small towns in rural or suburban Ohio towns where football had been the number one sport for decades. Attendance would usually range in the low hundreds to maybe a thousand for a big rivalry game. Games were almost always Saturdays at 1:00 p.m., for scheduling/travel reasons but also because many of the college stadiums, including Wooster (at the time), had no lights.

Anyway, all-aboard the Fighting Scot bus for the short 1-hour (assuming the bus made it) ride to Gambier, Ohio, to play the Kenyon Lords. I don't know if it was good or bad for me, as a freshman starter, to play my first two games on the road, away from the home crowd, under adverse conditions and no fans (no, we did *not* have a large traveling fan base . . .). In some way I think it helped me, because I wasn't able to get comfortable and had to be on my toes, alert for anything and everything without the benefit of familiarity. I was breaking in, and getting broken in, the hard way. But, as a one-game veteran, and with a win at that, I entered the game with a bit more confidence.

We were primarily a running team, and a basic power running team (no fancy wishbone option offense like we had at Baylor—didn't have the athletes for that at Wooster). We ran the ball whenever we could, and threw when we needed to. Our ground game worked well that day, and I left my second college game feeling good about our win (21-7) and my performance. Pig was playing a lot too—he was a very good running back (our leading rusher that year)—and that made our roommate experience even better. And when we won and were back on campus for a Saturday college night, we had a good time, and spirits were high.

Our third game, October 2, was also our first home game. Unlike most high schools, where pep rallies and other pre-game festivities were the norm for *every* football game—not so at college, apparently. Sure, we might wear our jerseys on Fridays before game day to show who we were, but I don't recall any other real outpouring of emotional support for the team other than the usually adequate, sometimes sparse, rarely overwhelming, attendance at home games (after all, students got in free!). But that is not to say that some students didn't take football a bit more seriously, or at least use it as a possible means to an end (like getting a date). And as I recall, it was sometime on Friday before our first home game when Mike and I answered a knocking on our Kenarden dorm door to find two or three young ladies with pom-poms (black and gold) there to "cheer" for us before our first home game. Well, Mike and I, young studly freshmen football players that we were, stood there gawking and smiling. One of them in particular caught my eye, a cute blonde I had seen on campus before and noticed (wonder how I might meet her sometime?). I'm sure Pig and I made some typically awkward freshman male remarks, laughed, and went back to doing whatever freshman guys do in college.

Finally, our first home game, an October Saturday on what I imagine was a spectacular early-fall day in Ohio, a great day to take our 2-0 record onto the field against the mighty Hiram Terriers. Our school colors were black and gold, with simple black helmets with a large "W" on each side. For home games, black jerseys on gold pants; for away games, white jerseys on gold pants (the pants didn't change in Division III football!).

The College of Wooster stadium is set in a slight depression right next to the student center and the phys ed center (also known as the PEC, or in collegiate slang the "PECer," with a hard "C," of course. Are you surprised?) on the east. It is bordered to the north by a hillside with trees and beautiful foliage in the fall, to the south, by the stadium bleachers (only on one side), and to the west, open space with the scoreboard. Really a picturesque spot for a fall afternoon of small college football, and one I could imagine being played out at dozens of similar venues across the USA, to some smaller and some much-larger crowds.

Wooster football tradition had the team assemble just outside the locker rooms in the PEC, above a small hill leading down to the stadium. Wooster had, and still has, a marching band, including Scottish bagpipes and kilts, which would lead the team down the hill where we would run out onto the field before our adoring—but scarce—fans. Well, some were adoring (on parents' weekend), but most were what I'd call "interested" spectators, a mix of (i) students who were actually up on a Saturday in time for lunch and figured a football game at 1:00 was as good a way as any to get their day started, (ii) faculty who had some interest in sports—and there were some (iii) Wooster residents, who liked the college and thought this was a great way to spend a Saturday afternoon, and (iv) parents, girlfriends, and other relatives of players who were in town that weekend, totaling, on a normal Saturday in the late 1970s, a few hundred people. As I said, I'd had bigger crowds in high school.

While it was my third college game, and third start, there was a special excitement about playing my first home game. Pig and I were up early for breakfast over at the student center. Back at the dorm we might try to study a little or go over the day's game plan, but by 10 a.m., we usually had my stereo cranked up with some extraordinarily loud rock 'n' roll (Boston, Outlaws, you get the idea) to get us more properly in the mood to play. Of course, for non-athletes in the dorm, the loud music early on a Saturday wasn't necessarily appreciated, but not many people were willing to ask us to turn it down—they knew this was part of the pre-game ritual, and such requests were generally denied. Over to the PEC about two hours before game time to dress, get taped, and be ready to take the field and warm-up by noon. Stretch as a team, some contact drills, run some plays, feel the adrenaline start to run through your body. A few looks over at the competition, trying to pick out (for me) their nose tackle, the guy I'd been watching on film all week and who I'd be trying to block. Back up the hill for the pre-game talk by our head coach, last-minute equipment adjustments, and then down the hill onto the field, now so pumped up I could hardly wait for first contact, knowing, always, that we should—that we would—win the game. And while it was by an unspectacular 9-6 margin, win the game we did. Celebration, 3-0, feeling like anything was possible this season. Bumps and bruises and pains melted away after a win and with some post-game Saturday night relaxation.

Whoever set up our schedule that year was not thinking too well. We only had three home games all year long—3 of 9. Unlike our first away game, these remaining games were all at other small colleges scattered around Ohio. Saturdays away meant packing the gear and loading the bus right after Saturday breakfast. Usually a stop along the way for something to eat—a not-very-nutritional pre-game meal. Arrive at the away "stadium" (in some cases more like a field with bleachers on one side), find the visitors' locker room, and get changed. The visitors' locker room was normally, at best, a set of rusty steel lockers on concrete, with too few benches. On one road trip I actually got changed in the weight room. Throw on the pads, get out and warm-up, play the game, shower (sometimes hot water), back on the bus, and the drive back to Wooster. If we would not make it back until after the student dining room had closed, and if our meager team budget allowed, we would stop at a McDonald's for dinner. If the coach wanted to reward us, maybe a Ponderosa Steak House all-you-can-eat salad bar and a $10 steak!

We were on the road that week against the Mount Union Purple Raiders . . . and lost 3-7. Then at the Muskingum Muskies . . . and were shut out 0-24. *Shut out!* That may have been the first time in my playing career that my offense had not scored. Then the next week, our arch-rival Wittenberg Tigers came in to *our* stadium and put a 33-0 pasting on us. Another shutout! Three losses in a row. A very new—and very unpleasant—experience for me. Up until this point, I had never been on a team that lost more than one game *in a season*—and here we were 3-3.

I felt I was getting better at my position, nevertheless. Learning different techniques, learning to lead the offensive line, even though I was just a freshman. Learning to play against men 2 and 3 years older than I was. I was big enough, but still not as grown into my body as many of these guys. We went back on the road the next week and eked out a win over the Heidelberg Student Princes (yes, that was their name). Then we lost our last two games to finish the worst season, record-wise, I had ever known: 4-5, a losing record. This continued the recent run of bad Wooster football teams and marked the end of the line for our head coach. Next year, we'd have a new head coach, though luckily for me, my line coach would be the same.

Between football and studies and occasional dates, first trimester at Wooster flew by. We were on a rather unique schedule where we had three trimesters, resulting in a long holiday break (Thanksgiving through New Year's), and not getting out for summer until early June. I wrapped up the first semester with good grades, a letter in football, and a great feeling about being in college in general and at Wooster in particular—I loved it. I never went home that first trimester—too hard to get there. I think my mom and dad, and maybe a brother or two, visited for parents' weekend, but not sure, and I'm not sure how these logistics would have worked, really. That cute blonde I mentioned a while back—her roommate set us up on a blind date that didn't go so well. Her name was Cindy Weiler, and she had intelligence and independence to go along with her Midwestern good looks. I later found out after our date she told her roommate I was a bust—she didn't want to see me again!

At Thanksgiving break, not having a car, I hitched a ride with a teammate who also lived in Tennessee, not far from Chattanooga. My dad met me in a small town and dropped me at home where my mom was still living in the big family house, with my two little brothers. It was strange to be back home, in and among all the family dynamics. It was good to see people, and be in a familiar place—but I realized it wasn't really my home anymore. I immediately went to work at the flour mill to make some spending money. Basically, my dad was paying for my college (room/board/tuition—$4,800/year), and I was responsible for everything else. We went through the usual holiday traditions—Thanksgiving breakfast at the church, off to my dad's parents in Sewanee, Tennessee, for Thanksgiving (Mom went to friends), split Christmas with Mom, and then with Dad and his new family (he would eventually remarry later in my freshman year). After 5 weeks of hard work at the mill, and family, I was ready to get back to my college home.

Before slipping back to my first winter in Ohio and leaving the Tennessee holidays, I really should expand on one of those holiday traditions: the annual tradition of stealing the family Christmas tree. Now, I've written about my parents' ethics, and in particular, my dad's usually scrupulous views of right and wrong . . . which held up under *most* circumstances and normal rationalized scrutiny. But for some reason, and this is something I didn't think about until *after* many years of executing the strategy, this did not apply when it came time to find our family Christmas tree. From the time we moved to Signal Mountain, which at that time was admittedly on the fringe of "rural" and "unsettled," we (meaning dad, me, and any brother(s) old enough) would load into a car (usually the fabled yellow Ford Maverick or beige Chevy Nomad wagon) with saw, ax, and gloves. We drove up to the top of the mountain along the road several miles until we seemed to be in the middle of nowhere. Just the two-lane road, pine and other trees, some shack-like homes, and a few "no trespassing" signs.

There was a dirt road off to one side where we'd turn in, drive a couple hundred yards off the main road, and then go Christmas tree hunting. Once the candidate was located, sawed or hacked down, strapped to the car or in the car (often with one of my little brothers complaining about the branch sticking him in the side or face), we'd cruise back down to our place and erect the 12–15-foot "free" tree in our living room. The last time I participated in this misdemeanor tradition was that first Christmas back from college, where we also took one of my favorite pictures with my brothers.

The tradition ended the very next year, though I was not in attendance. As the story is told by my brother Bob, this time as the three of them were thrashing through the trees with their freshly cut prize, and tying it to the car, a "local" with a shotgun approached and asked what the hell they were doing on private property, taking a tree out. My dad, employing his best lawyerly verbal skills, talked their way into the car and off the property, George complaining about the needles in his face, and Bob telling him to shut up. That was the last of the free Christmas trees . . .

I arrived back in Wooster, Ohio, for my first real winter (Tennessee winters don't count). For me, that meant switching from the usual tennis shoes, jeans, and T-shirt, to work boots, jeans, T-shirt, and sweatshirt with a heavy flannel coat and a stocking cap. Not too well prepared, this Southern boy. Wooster is on the southern edge of the Great Lakes Snowbelt, so we got our fair share of snow, and it was cold! Of course, that created new opportunities, like night tubing down the nearby park hillside, certainly not a Tennessee tradition. It may have been the first time I'd ever seen snow skis in person (cross-country), not sports equipment I'd seen in Chattanooga.

I tried to schedule my classes early in the mornings so that I was finished with class by lunch. Ideally, I'd have an 8 a.m. class, and one or two others in the morning. That left the afternoon open to study, do science labs (yes, still "premed"), and work out. In Division III football, there can be no organized formal off-season training program. And in this era, at Wooster and other colleges like it, I can assure you there was no informal program either. Many football players still did not train year-round, as they do today, and many still did not lift weights in any serious way. Not so for me—the off-season was my time for getting bigger and stronger.

When I first walked into the College of Wooster "weight room," I realized this would be a challenge. Picture a moderate-sized room, linoleum flooring, some mats over against one wall, and in the middle of the room a universal gym, vintage: old. A universal gym, for those of you too young to know, was a massive assortment of plates, cables, pulleys, and bars, which purportedly allowed one to exercise every major muscle group by using different stations around the machine. Perhaps six–eight people could use it simultaneously. No dumbbells, no free weights, no bench press (which to a football player then was the weight lifting standard). With some encouragement of the coaching staff, we were able to get an actual set of free weights in there, but they were not what you'd call Olympic-style weights, but rather retail—thin bar, thin plates, thinly padded, and small bench press (which is a problem when you are trying to use a lot of weight). But I made do with what was there, implementing my own regimen of heavy lifting three times a week (religiously), and on other days doing something aerobic. I preferred basketball, full court when I could get a game, or racquetball with Pig or whoever I could find.

And I ate, and ate, and drank milk, and drank milk. And trained. I was not sure at the time what was driving me, except I knew I wanted to be better, bigger, and stronger. I pushed myself to build on my freshman year. I wanted to be the best center Wooster had ever had. And I wanted to win, figuring if I was the best I could be, then surely we would win more. I was not going to endure another losing season—it was horrible to me.

Pig worked out with me much of the time. He was also driven. But he was also a very good baseball player, and in midwinter that sport pulled him away. There were a few other football players who would spend time in the weight room, but not many and not all the time. For me, it was part of life. Mid-afternoon on a cold winter day, put on the sweats, stocking cap, trudge through the cold and snow to the PEC, work out hard for at least an hour, and then back to the dorm, shower, dinner, study. Repeat.

But that wasn't my whole life, of course. I was working hard in class, breaking glassware in chemistry lab (when my dad got that bill—he sent it to *me*), hitting a few parties, and dating lightly. And then Cindy's roommate, who ignored Cindy's admonition after date #1 with me to "never do that again," set us up again on "blind" date number two. Blind to Cindy, because until she saw me she thought it would be someone else—*anyone* else. But once there, she was stuck on another date with me. And this time I must have done something right (persistence?), because we clicked and agreed to start going out. Well, to be fair, I readily agreed; I think she relented. And soon after that, I had fallen in love and that was that. The best thing to ever happen to me happened when I was 18, that spring, when I fell in love with the woman who would eventually spend the next 37 years (and counting) with me. But in the winter/spring of 1977, we didn't know all that, and we were just two 18/19 year olds in love, in college, having a great time.

Whether from competitive boredom or otherwise, when the winter finally broke and spring came to Wooster, I decided to join the track team, though mainly as a structured way to further my off-season conditioning program but allow for some competition. I mainly threw the discus (which I had done at Baylor), tinkered with some shot put, and used the warm afternoons to run, condition, and lift. The track coach, the wonderful Coach Phil Shipe, understood what I was doing, and gave me plenty of latitude to design my own training program, which included leaving practice to go lift weights, whenever I wanted to. I never achieved any great results as a "track man," but did place in the discus in a few meets, garnering the team a few points here and there. Even with this relaxed approach (and very little coaching), given my sheer size and strength at this level, I was the #1 or #2 discus guy for Wooster each year, and competitive in meets. Very little skill, just throw the damn thing out there. But I did work at it and became a passable discus man.

Spring passed quickly, with classes, Cindy, and social activities occupying most of my time. Wooster did not have a system of national fraternities, but instead, lower-key "local" fraternities, and Pig and I and a few other friends decided to join one. That involved something called "hell week," or the pledge week, which I hated but did. Looking back, it's one of those things you do as an 18-year-old trying to fit in. Seemed important at the time. But it was really more about choosing a group of guys to live with in a dormitory for the next three years (remember—all-male dorms).

What a freshman year! Starting on the football team was great, despite the losing record. My new friends, Cindy, freedom, classes— my new life. I loved it, felt I was becoming "Blake Moore." I even had my first car, a bright red VW Super Beetle, which somewhat counterintuitively was a good physical fit for me because of the high, rounded shape. I bought the car with my hard-earned savings from all those summers of mowing lawns, cleaning dog crap, and sweating in the flour mill. And I bought it on spring break, after doing the trip home that time by Greyhound bus—a tortuous, cigarette smoke-filled, uncomfortable 16-hour journey during which I made up my mind: never again!

Back to Chattanooga for the summer, and back to work.

Summer with my Wooster schedule only meant about 9–10 weeks. With my girlfriend back in Minnesota for her summer, and not many social or other activities that interested me on Signal Mountain, it meant I went straight back to work at the flour mill. Punch the clock at 7 a.m., work and sweat all day long with half an hour for lunch, punch out at 3:30, and drive my flour-coated red VW straight to Baylor. With school out, most facilities were closed, but that didn't slow me down. I crawled under or over the fence to the football stadium and created my own interval training workout that involved running, sprinting, jumping rope, and stadium steps. And when I say stadium steps, I don't mean just running up and down. Sure, I sprinted up, but I also did the steps backward and sideways, adding to the footwork difficulty. And I was doing this in the heat of the Chattanooga day, usually 85–95 degrees.

From there, three times a week, I would find my way into the Baylor weight room, which was actually better than the Wooster weight room in terms of equipment. I had a full range of free weights, bars, and benches, and in those days, free weights, heavy lifting in sets of three, progressively adding weight, was the way football players (those who lifted) trained. I would put myself through a good lifting routine, almost always alone. At some point, Baylor even bought a newfangled strength machine called a "Nautilus," which was an inquisition-like contraption, blue steel, that purported to be an entire chest and shoulder machine. It was so new it was generally kept locked up behind a cage fence, but I quickly solved that by scaling the fence and crawling through the gap between fence and ceiling. I had to use that machine. I had to get stronger. I was focused on making sure never to repeat that losing record again, even if, by God, I had to do it myself.

After the day of work and my workout, exhausted, I would head home, eat dinner, read, write Cindy a letter, go to bed, get up, and do it again. One or two times a week would be the somewhat awkward dinner or activity with my brothers and my dad and his family. I realized my brothers were doing this all year, not just like me on my college breaks. Even though we three were all impacted by the divorce, I recognize that from a day-to-day standpoint, I had avoided much of the everyday logistics of it by being away at college.

When that summer ended, I was ready physically and mentally to get back to Wooster. Physically, I had added weight and was reporting to camp at 230 pounds, in the best shape I'd ever been in, and stronger than I'd ever been. I had pushed myself, and it showed. Mentally, I was back at Wooster most of the summer, missing Cindy, my friends, and college life in general.

Our new head coach Tom Holman came in fired up and ready too. He was a more emotional, fiery coach than our former head coach, and more than any of my previous head coaches. He was prone to getting going on some pretty good rants. We could tell whenever he'd been going for a while, as a small but persistent piece of white spittle would form on his lower lip. Those of us in the front row—and that's where we team leaders sat—were more concerned about that piece of spit flying off and hitting us than what he was saying. He did have some memorable lines, like: "Men—life is like a rolly [sic] coaster: sometimes you're up high (motioning with hands), and sometimes you're down low." Can't even remember what the point of this one was, except we all joked about the "rolly coaster" for years. He also posted motivational stuff on the locker room board like many coaches do. One of my favorites, and I still use it often: *Luck is when preparation meets with opportunity*. Fit my work-hard-to-succeed philosophy perfectly.

I think we all knew Coach Holman was a little different as we prepared for our first game. To help get the team thinking as a team and get us fired up, the night before our first game he marched us all in, Friday night, to the campus movie theater, where we watched Spartacus, who in 3½ hours of bloody, gladiatorial uprising glory, played the role of the consummate underdog who never gives up. Corny as it was, he was sending us a clear message—together, if we decided to, we could do anything. Even defeat the Romans.

I will spare you a game-by-game summary of the next three seasons and rather hit some highlights and meaningful events that helped define my college, football, and life experience. We started that 1977 season 3-0, and we were feeling good. Several of our freshman class, now sophomores, were starting or playing a lot. We knew better what we were doing, and what we wanted to do.

As the returning starting center, I stepped in to much more of a leadership role with the offensive line and the team. Our line coach gave me more latitude at the line to make calls. We developed that year and ensuing years a whole language of our own to make our blocking calls. For example, if we wanted to double team the nose tackle, we would call "Downtown" (DT for "double team"), "New Orleans" (being a famous "downtown" city), or eventually evolving, as it inevitably had to, to "whore house," which were (we had heard) plentiful in downtowns like New Orleans. So during the course of the game, I and other linemen could be heard screaming "Whore house! Whore house!" while the quarterback was in his snap count. I can only imagine what the refs and the other team thought of that.

The other quite memorable event of the August training camp was reuniting with Cindy after a summer away. She was back earlier than the other students, as she was working a campus advisory job. Our practices were held often in a large grass field surrounded by dorms, one of which was where she'd be living her sophomore year. As we were jogging up to practice another hot day, I looked up and saw her personal note to me that she was back in town: she'd strategically hung a pair of bright red/white-checked underwear out her window. I went through a very energized practice with a smile on my face! And somewhere I still have that underwear, kept all these years.

This fall of 1977 was also the first time I would meet Cindy's parents, Phil and Barb. Phil was a Presbyterian minister (I had also been "raised" Presbyterian), and they were coming down for parents' weekend to see Cindy, meet me, and watch a football game (both Phil and Barb were big Vikings fans). I can't remember a thing about the Saturday home game, but sure do remember that evening. I was nervous as hell! Cindy later told me *her* parents were nervous to meet me—funny.

We had reservations at the Smithville Inn, a 20-minute drive from Wooster, a nice family dinner out where I could be scrutinized by Cindy's parents. I believe one or two siblings were along too (she had three sisters and a brother, all younger). I had my VW all shined and bright red, and led the way down the country road, Phil and Barb and family following close behind. So far so good. But about 10 minutes out (and that's all it took to be in the "country" from Wooster), my car started acting funny. I looked in the rearview mirror and saw gray-black smoke billowing out of my engine, flowing back into and nearly obscuring the Weilers' car. What the hell?!

I pulled over to the side of the road, realizing we'd have to tow the car. About that time, I also realized I had *no cash* on me, planning to use a credit card for dinner. So, one of my first interactions with my future father-in-law was to have to ask him if I could borrow $20 for the tow. I was mortified, though as Cindy put it later, my having to ask Phil for a favor actually put him at ease with me. The rest of dinner must have gone fine, as I later managed to get an invite to their house for Christmas, in northern Minnesota (Crookston).

That fall also saw my plans to become a doctor wind down. The afternoon science labs were wearing me out, and I wanted that time for football, training, and other important "stuff." After slogging through basic chemistry, Organic Chemistry I and II, Biology of Cells (a B minus! I was horrified), I finally threw in the towel and decided to do something I thought I'd never do: major in history. My high school experience with history was boring—a seeming recitation and memorization of old facts and dates. However, history in college was a very different proposition, taught in a way that captured my interest and imagination. I liked it! It also gave me the time flexibility I wanted to take other courses and do other things.

We ended that season 6-3, losing one or two we should have won, but better as a team, and a winning record felt a helluva lot better than 4-5 felt. I was also recognized somewhat surprisingly by getting first-team all-conference honors at center. Surprising because I was only a sophomore. And, of course, for me, once *that* bar was set, there was no going back: I would have to work harder to be better, more successful the next year. Translation: I got even more serious about my training and weight lifting in the off-season. Five or 6 days a week. Every week. Lift hard three times a week. Every week. The competition was working hard—I would work harder.

As mentioned, I was invited to join Cindy and her family for Christmas in northern Minnesota that winter. Northern Minnesota? This Tennessee boy thought *Ohio* was north! In preparation, Cindy insisted on buying me a proper down-filled winter coat, suitable for 0 degrees. My flannel jacket wouldn't cut it in Crookston. Flying in over snow-covered North Dakota (flying to Crookston usually meant landing in Fargo or Grand Forks) terrain, it looked like the snow went on forever, flat white nothingness. Cindy picked me up at the airport in one of her family's fleet of vehicles (they had two Ford Pintos, a huge station wagon cruiser, and at least two snowmobiles). The drive of about 90 minutes did nothing to change my perspective on my surroundings: white, cold, and flat. It was somewhere around 10 below zero. In the course of my visit, the temperature never went *above* zero, and was regularly 20 or 30 below at night. I distinctly remember on our drive from the airport back to Cindy's house, her saying: "Here is *the* curve." "Here is *the* hill." Meaning, literally, there was *one* curve and *one* hill over that drive to her place just outside of Crookston. Made Ohio look like the Rocky Mountains it was so flat. When we pulled into her driveway, I noticed off to the side, buried in a snowbank so that only the tip of its antennae protruded, another car that would sit there until the snow melted (if it ever did!).

I was overwhelmed by the cold—and the need to be prepared for it when going outside. Of course, there was the issue of figuring out where and how I would get my workouts in. Occasionally, when it warmed up enough (near zero), I would venture out and run up and down the snow-packed country road and jump rope in the iced stillness of the day. Other times I'd hitch a ride into Crookston and exercise at Cindy's dad's church—running around their linoleum auditorium—I think about 25 laps was a mile. On one trip into town, in one of the mighty Pintos, I noticed that even after driving a while the car wouldn't warm up, and there was a persistent draft of cold air coming in around my feet. Looking down, staring, I finally realized I was seeing the *road*, or more properly snow/ice, through holes in the flooring that had rusted through with salt and snow and ice.

Finally the day came for the big family road trip. All of us (seven Weilers, plus me) loaded into the station wagon cruiser and headed—get this—*north!* Right, *further* north. In fact, not just north, but into Canada, to Winnipeg, three hours north. The border crossing comprised a small nondescript building, a cold border guard, and a perfunctory nod of the head. No ID required. Our destination in Winnipeg: Mother Tuckers, a then-famous restaurant known to Cindy's parents as the place where one could pay one price and get all the prime rib and side dishes we could eat; known to the locals there in Winnipeg for its play on words, which, looking back, I find particularly funny: my future father-in-law minister took us all to a place irreverently called "Mother Tuckers." Great stuff. Oh, and after dinner? We all loaded back into the car and drove back home. What an adventure. But also a warm memory from a very cold place.

That winter of 1978 in Ohio turned out to be one of the coldest ever, and snowiest. When Cindy and I landed in Cleveland to get back to school from Christmas break, the old VW barely started, and then about halfway between Cleveland and Wooster, on the interstate highway, it basically froze up and quit it was so cold outside.

We huddled in the car until the Highway Patrol stopped and picked us up, and by now it was dark. From the HP headquarters I phoned good friend and teammate George Anderson to make the emergency run up to get us in his car. The VW sat by the side of the road until the next day, when I recruited another offensive lineman who had a large van to drive up and hook a 10-foot cable to his rear bumper and my front bumper (no way I could afford the 30-mile professional tow). I put the VW in neutral, and steered and applied the brakes to keep the cable taut, all the way back to Wooster and the repair shop. Amazing the foolish things we do when 20 years old—and never even stopped to think about it too much! Of course, that's the secret—don't think. That experience pretty much doomed the VW, and it was eventually replaced with a snazzy Chevy Monza (old folks remember; young folks are furiously googling "Monza"). With bucket seats and a hatch-back (Monza 2+2). Cruisin'.

My sophomore year passed quickly. That winter of 1978 actually closed the college for two days, first time in over half a century, due to a blizzard that eventually blew up into Boston and helped form the worst nor'easter they've ever had. The school year was full of classes, social activities, and parties (which, with a girlfriend, was great), and, of course, working out every day, playing basketball and racquetball to stay in shape. Cindy decided to stay in Wooster for the summer, while I felt I had to go home where I had a job and see my family. For me it was back to the flour mill and the same tortuous workout regime I had developed the prior year. With Cindy 600 miles away and no real social life to speak of in Chattanooga, I threw myself into my routine with a vengeance. No day was too hot. I refused to cut short a workout even on the worst days. I pushed myself, and I mean myself. There was no coach, no trainer, no teammate to push me. It was me, the stadium steps, the 100-degree track, and the weight room. When I finished up my training to head back to Wooster at the end of the summer, I felt unstoppable, at 6 foot 5, and 240 pounds. And that would make me one of the biggest linemen in the Ohio Athletic Conference of Division III colleges—and my goal was to be not just one of the biggest, but the best.

I was excited to be back on campus early, and back with Cindy. And the rest of the football team was there, so it was kind of like this small group of us "owned" the campus for a couple weeks. Optimism always runs high during training camp—new season, new start, fresh new players to add to the veteran mix. This to contrast with the grind of camp, the two-a-days (full pads, full contact, two hours in the morning and two more in the afternoon) with meetings sandwiched in amongst meals and practices. We knew Coach Holman, and he knew us. It was my third year with my line coach, Art Marangi, and he and I had developed a trust and rapport that empowered me to be even better. I had input in blocking schemes, and play-calling on the sidelines. Again, we started fast out of the blocks, running our record to 3-0. The ultimate prize then, and now, for a Division III football player, was to make the NCAA playoffs and ultimately play in the championship game, the Amos Alonzo Stagg Bowl, named for one of the winningest college football coaches of all time. We talked about it, talked about making it to that game as our goal. And we had the season off to the start we needed.

Recall our Coach Holman was the motivational type. One of our regular opponents each year was Muskingam College, another small Ohio college nestled in a picturesque small town. I remember playing at Muskingam my freshman year and driving down into their campus on a perfect fall day, leaves orange/gold/red, piling out of the bus in the crisp air, just dying to get out on the field and play football. Days like that made me love the game. Anyway, we had developed a very poor record against the Muskingam "Fighting Muskies," and Coach Holman was tired of it. Wooster hadn't beaten them since 1947. *1947!* And Coach Holman decided this was the year to end *that* streak. He gathered the team around him on the practice field, under the goal post. He went into a spittle-laced rant about Muskingam College, those "Muskies," and our losing streak. And that streak was going to end with us, this week, on Saturday. Whereupon he pulled out a dead fish, proclaiming it was a Muskie (I believe that actually is a kind of fish), and hung it upside down by a string from the goal post. All week long during practice it hung there. All week long we heard about the streak. And on Friday, our final practice before the game, he cut the smelly, rotten Muskie down and buried it right on the field, telling us that was what we were going to do to the Muskingam Muskies, and that damn streak—bury them! And we roared our approval, and with that "bury the Muskies" rant in our heads and on our lips on Saturday, we went out and did just that, 21-10.

One of the road trips I'll never forget was on an October day in 1978, junior year. We were on the road to play at Otterbein, a couple of hours over rolling country roads. We set out on the mighty Scot team bus, with the usual equipment van behind us. We were about an hour into our trip, sitting peacefully on the bus, casual banter by some players, others getting focused on the game to come. Suddenly, cruising along at about 50 mph, the bus hesitated, accompanied by a horrific grinding and screeching of metal on metal. We lurched forward and eventually came to a stop on the side of the road. We stumbled off the bus, and there on the road, stretching back for a quarter of a mile, were what appeared to be the entire drivetrain and engine, scattered in a smear of oil, grease, and parts all over the road. We milled around, wondering what we'd do. We hadn't built this into our schedule. Eventually a backup bus, I think a yellow school bus, picked us up, and we got to Otterbein just shortly before game time, threw on our gear, did a quick warm-up, and went out and played. Classic Division III experience!

As my dedication and commitment to the game of football developed over the years physically, so too did my emotional and mental commitment. All serious athletes develop ways to get into the right frame of mind to play their game. Football is, at its base level, a physically violent game of one-on-one competition, especially in the line play. My goal, every play, was to impose my will physically on my opponent. Every down, every play. Sure, there are complex plays and strategies and blocking assignments, but when the ball is snapped, all that remains is to beat the guy in front of you. Hit him in the chest, cut his knees out from under him, blindside him, put him on his back, drive him into the ground.

I found that to get ready for this, I had to get my mind focused in a way I didn't do for any other activity. I found a quiet spot away from all the pre-game activity, in view of the field. I visualized the other team, my opponent, his number, and how I was going to dominate him. I could feel the adrenaline start to flow into my system . . . was as alive as anyone could possibly be. Completely focused on the next three hours of my life and nothing else. Sometimes the emotional intensity was so severe I would cry, overwhelmed by the energy, the desire to win. Then with total focus of mind and purpose, I'd rejoin my team, and take the field. You've heard the saying about being ready to run through a brick wall? I was ready.

Junior year season (1978) ended with a 6-3 record. We couldn't quite get to that next level, the conference championship that would give us a shot at the Stagg Bowl. While our record was disappointing, individually I was recognized all-conference again, and then also won the Dick Gregory award, given to the top lineman in the conference. I was quite pleased with that, and I even was recognized as honorable mention Little All-American ("Little" for small colleges). I had raised the bar on my play and expectations—no going back.

The rest of my junior year was similar to my sophomore year. Winter in Ohio, classes, normal college social activities, Cindy, working out at the PEC. As it got toward spring again, I realized I didn't want to leave Wooster that summer, mainly because Cindy was staying there, but also because I was really "done" with my life in Chattanooga. Pig also decided to stay, so we found an old house to rent for the summer, near campus. Our rent? Paint the outside of the house over the course of the summer. Of course, I needed to get a job to make some money to support all those college activities, and here is where I should introduce a person who probably made the biggest impact on my football life—more than my coaches, more than my parents, more than any person other than myself.

Ernie Infield when I met him was the sports information director for the College of Wooster. His job was to write about, document, promote, and publicize College of Wooster athletics generally. He was also a journalist of many years, who wrote a regular column in the Wooster (city) newspaper, the *Daily Record,* captioned "Ramblin' Round the Infield," an obvious play on his last name. Ernie was also an accomplished and unashamed punster, so this suited his style. An ex-marine, buzz-cut happy man who loved the College of Wooster, sports, his family, his farm, and what he did for a living.

Ernie watched my early progress on the football team and realized (probably before me) that I might be a little different from most other players who had played at Wooster since 1889. He took a personal interest in me, started giving me some good local publicity. He also helped me find that summer job in 1978, lining me up to work for one of his friends (Ken Miller) who owned an oil pipe yard just outside Wooster. Ernie kept track of my career at Wooster and my development. He talked to me about the history of Wooster football, the background of the Dick Gregory award, and other Wooster football legends like John Papp, Tom Dingle, and Bob Macoritti—who Ernie told me was the only Wooster player to ever play professional football (though not exactly accurate)— in the Canadian Football League as a kicker. Ernie had a deep respect for the game, and all components of it. He would remind me from time to time of the importance of being a good long snapper as a center, a skill that very few players ever developed, but that *every* team needed.

Now about that summer job. From the stiflingly hot flour mill, into the fire. I was a basic laborer in the pipe yard. Oil and gas extraction was a pretty big business in that part of Ohio in those days (not like Texas, but the black stuff was down there), and scattered all over this region of Ohio were small oil wells and drilling rigs. All those required pipe and drilling equipment, and that is what Ken Miller Pipe did. I worked outside in the sun all day, moving, loading, and unloading steel pipe on and off trucks. Eight hours a day. The pipe could be long and slender, maybe 2 inches in diameter, or it could be 12 inches, and extremely heavy. I drove trucks around the yard, learned to operate a forklift (not very well, but passable), and was covered in sweat and pipe grease at the end of every day. Working steel pipe has its dangers, like catching a hand or a finger in a pile, or getting twisted up in a pile of pipe that rolled off its stack. One time when I was climbing around a stack of pipe, and several rolled down and pinned my ankle (painfully), my foreman looked at me and said, without a smile: "You gotta be smarter than the pipe." *You gotta be smarter than the pipe.* Genius! I've used that saying on myself, others, and my kids hundreds of times over the years. So much wisdom in seven words. You gotta be smarter than the pipe. Who knew I'd learn a life lesson in the oil pipe yard . . .

Ernie Infield, over the years as a sports writer in Ohio, had gathered quite a few contacts in the business. Probably most notable among them was a multi-decade professional friendship with Paul Brown, Ohio high school and NFL coaching legend. Paul Brown had founded the Cleveland Browns many years prior, had left there, and then founded (in 1968) the Cincinnati Bengals. Ernie had known Paul (and eventually his son Mike) for years, first covering Paul's legendary high school teams, then the Browns, and now the Bengals. Each year, Ernie would create a preseason spread in the *Wooster Daily Record* on the Cincinnati Bengals. He had an open invitation from Paul Brown himself to every Bengals preseason training camp, to walk "inside the ropes," interview any players he chose, and get a private audience with Paul and Mike. Pretty heady stuff for a small-town reporter, but Paul knew Ernie was a professional and treated him as well, or better than, any reporter from a big newspaper.

A few weeks into my summer at Ken Miller Pipe, Ernie announced "we" would be going down to the Bengals training camp in early August to meet Paul, Mike, and some players. Bear in mind I had never even been to an NFL game in my life, much less been up close with any professional players. I hadn't really harbored any dreams of playing in the NFL, either, though my constant drive to "get better" every year was certainly producing results. Sure I had been a lifetime fan and watched games every weekend. As I got to be as big as some of the linemen playing in the NFL, yes, I sometimes thought to myself: *I can do that—I can be that good.* But it was never a dream or something I thought too seriously about . . . until Ernie announced we were going to visit the Bengals.

I've mentioned my summer workout regimen when home in Chattanooga. This summer in Wooster, after getting off work at the pipe yard, I would drive my Chevy Monza (2+2) over to the college for my late-afternoon workouts. Once again, my goal was to be bigger and stronger than the year before. I wanted to gain another 10 pounds of muscle, and my goal was to play my senior year at 250 pounds. So when Ernie said we'd be going down to see the Bengals in August, I was ready. Best shape of my life, bigger and stronger than I'd ever been, and at 6 foot 5, 250 pounds, I knew I was around the size of many NFL offensive linemen.

We loaded up Ken Miller's Cadillac sedan, me as chauffeur, Ken and Ernie in the back, old friends telling stories. I had no idea what to expect. For starters, I think it was the first time I'd ever been in a Cadillac! We drove two hours or so down south to Wilmington, Ohio, a small town outside Cincinnati where the Bengals set up training camp each year at Wilmington College (a small college which, at that time, was not unlike Wooster, even smaller). We rolled onto campus, and Ernie took over, checking out our schedule with the Bengals PR man. It was a whirlwind of a day.

I tagged along as Ernie interviewed a few players, and Paul and Mike Brown. We went to lunch in the players' cafeteria, and I got to see them amble in after morning practice for lunch, some bigger than me, many smaller. We went out to watch the afternoon practice, and Ernie had a special spot right alongside Paul Brown for the practice. At one point Paul even called over their starting center, Blair Bush, to introduce us. We shook hands, Bush in full gear, full sweat, me basically sizing him up. Ernie watched the brief interaction and just smiled. Before we left that afternoon, I'd also been introduced to one of the Bengals senior scouts, who was, I am sure, sizing *me* up. Ernie left Paul with a little comment along the lines of "keep an eye on this kid—he's pretty good," and then we were back in the Cadillac and up the highway to Wooster.

On the trip back and the rest of that summer, I considered what I'd just done and seen. It was the first time I really, seriously, considered that I could play professional football in the NFL. I had seen the players up close, watched what they were doing, and mentally compared what they were doing to what I *believed* I could do. It was surely still a remote possibility, and one I wouldn't count on, but for the first time, it settled into my head as another goal, however distant, to aim for. I decided that summer that I wanted a shot—just a shot—and that became yet another motivating factor during the hot summer weeks in the weight room and on the track, mentally and physically preparing myself for my last season at Wooster.

Summer passed. Pig and I paid our "rent" by applying one or two coats of cheap paint to the house. Another lesson learned—I'd never be a professional house painter. When we were done, it was tough to tell we had painted it . . . But I look back on that summer fondly. First time I'd been "on my own" living (not in a college dorm with college food). Kept my own schedule, hung out with Cindy, worked, worked out, ate what we wanted, and drank cold beer with Pig after an intense workout. By the time training camp rolled around, Pig and I felt we were ready for a breakout year. Along with my roommate the prior year, George Anderson, the three of us felt we and the other seniors (and there were only eight left!) were primed to break out of 6-3 mode and win our conference. This was going to be *our* year.

But as our first game approached, things weren't going as perfectly as I'd hoped. A few days before the game, I got some virus that wouldn't go away, and I had the worst diarrhea of my life. Nothing would stay in, and I lost weight and strength and fluid. The trainer and doctor weren't sure what to do. I kept practicing, because I was stubborn, and as a senior and captain, I wasn't going to miss this for anything. But come game time, even with various antidiarrheal medication and remedies, I was still "fluid." That is definitely a problem when you are playing football, and every play you are to explode *into* your opponent. It is hard to do that *and* keep tight pucker control on the other end, but I was determined to do it. Certainly one of the toughest games for me in college. Their nose tackle was about 5 foot 8, 220 pounds, a fire hydrant, and I was 6 foot 5, trying to get low and leverage on him all game long. And try to keep my insides from spilling into my pants. I was more successful than not on the former, and marginally successful on the latter (including a required halftime change of gear). Though we won, I was exhausted and felt I had played just average—not the way I wanted to start my senior year.

We managed a 4-1 start to the year, and that set up our big home game against the 5-0 Wittenberg Tigers, our arch-nemesis, a team that had beaten us every year. A win at home and we would be in the driver's seat for the conference title, and that chance for the playoff run to the Amos Alonzo Stagg Bowl. We were as high as we could be for the game, the stadium was full that day, and the Scot band led us onto the field—where everything proceeded to go wrong, and we got our asses kicked 35-6. That was tough to take, not just because we were beaten so badly, but also because it basically took us out of the title chase. And it led ultimately to another 6-3 season.

Our last game was at home against Mount Union, my last time to wear the Black and Gold, my number 52. It was cold, raining, muddy, and a loss. I remember trudging back up the hill to the locker room after the game, soaked and cold and muddy and disappointed. And then I just sat on the bench, in full gear, in front of my old steel locker, and cried. And stared ahead. And cried. I couldn't bring myself to take off my pads. What if this was my last game? What if I never played football again? Never had a team again, the camaraderie, the adrenaline, the battle, the intensity, the winning and losing? I had not prepared myself for this. I wasn't ready.

The rest of the team cleaned up and cleared out. I sat in my muddy uniform and thought all these thoughts. I wasn't ready for it to be over. Whether it was in that long stare into my locker, or in the days that followed, I resolved to myself that I wasn't done, that I wanted a shot at the next level, and I would work to make that happen. I just wanted a shot.

I was fortunate to be recognized again for my accomplishments on the field. All-Conference, the Gregory award (not sure how many players ever won this back-to-back), and first-team little All-American, as well as an NCAA scholarship to be used toward graduate school in recognition of my Academic All-American status (yeah, I had kept my grades up throughout college). All these were gratifying, and I was pleased, but in my head I was thinking *What next? I am not satisfied!*

Winter of my senior year was an academic push. At Wooster, every senior is required to spend most of his or her senior year on something called IS, or Independent Study. This is the capstone work for any Wooster grad and is a research/writing project done in one's major, with a professor acting as advisor and critic on the project. Mine, of course, was in my major, history, and was on the subject of Leonid Brezhnev's Soviet Union. It required many hours in the library on cold winter days, poring through card catalogs (young readers— Google "card catalog"), obscure publications and journals, and then hours of drafting, writing, and rewriting in my dorm room. This was the main academic workload, along with a few other classes in senior year. And, of course, senior year is senior year—a year of celebration with longtime friends that college is almost over, not really realizing that about 20 years later many of us would realize it may have been the best four years of our lives. Cindy was a constant in my life, and we'd been engaged now for over a year, with no definite wedding plans—we had just decided we were committed to each other. So I spent most of my senior year "in residence" with Cindy at her place, with only daily pit stops at my dorm room.

The Bengals and Paul Brown kept their word, and as Ernie Infield predicted, the Bengals sent their head scout up to "officially" scout me for the team. Scouting season in the NFL is normally (or was, at that time) a player's senior college football season, where scouts would come watch them play, or watch them on TV. Not a lot of TV coverage for the Fighting Scots, and I'm pretty sure there was never an

NFL scout at one of my games. But on a cold winter day, the Bengal scout drove onto campus, with a couple days' notice by phone call. We met in the gym, me in shorts, T-shirt, tennis shoes—not really having any idea what a scout would "scout." He took the normal measurements, like height (6 foot 5) and weight (250 pounds), and then some others I wasn't used to, like arm length. He ran me through some agility drills, measured my flexibility, had me do some vertical jumps. And, of course, he wanted to see me long-snap, both for punts (15 yards) and field goals (7 yards). With some nervousness, I completed all the drills, sweating, out of breath. He thanked me and told me to keep working on the long snapping, and they'd be in touch.

Now, even in those days, the NFL was a "copycat" league, and if one team looked at a player, well, sure as hell, others would too. Must be the scouts' grapevine. Before long, I had letters from the Cleveland Browns, Seattle Seahawks, and maybe one or two others. They were "interested" and wanted to come scout me too. They all had me perform very similar drills and tests. I recall the scout from Seattle complaining he'd gotten lost trying to find Wooster, as he'd never been there before. *Really?* They took their notes, made their observations, and usually gave me a couple of pointers on things to work on. I would ask a few questions and focus on doing the tests as well as I could. The one area they all talked about was the long-snapping skill. Why? Keep in mind that in this era each NFL team had 45 players—only 45. No practice squad, no scout team. With that number, specialized skills such as long snapping had to be done by one of the 45 who also could play one or more "normal" positions, like offensive line or linebacker. There was no concept of having a player on the team whose only job was long snapping. The only two specialists carried on any team were the punter and kicker, and some coaches didn't even like doing that.

I took the not-so-subtle advice to heart, and working on my long snapping became part of my winter workout regimen. Yes, I had handled all the long-snapping responsibilities in high school, and for every one of my 36 college games. I knew how to do it. But the

NFL skill was a different level, requiring more speed, more accuracy, better timing. I got Pig to catch for me on some days at the gym after a weight workout or racquetball session. I kept balls in my dorm room, and at times I'd grab a hall mate (usually sober) and position them at one end of the narrow dorm hallway. I'd go to the other end, and have about 14 yards to work with. High snaps smashed into the "EXIT" sign, and by the end of the winter it was kind of loose—not all my snaps were perfect! But the discipline of practicing all off-season was important. With the scouts appearing, my resolve to get a shot at the NFL took on a sense of reality. If I worked hard enough, surely I'd get a chance, maybe even get drafted. I compared myself to some of the other college linemen I was reading about. I had the size, but, of course, I was a starter at Wooster, not at Tennessee, or Alabama, or Nebraska. In the normal world of NFL prospects, it was a miracle I was even on the radar screen, traced back to that summer trip with Ernie Infield to visit the Bengals. But I was on the edge of that radar screen, a distant but insistent blip.

Senior year ended for me after winter semester. With my AP credits, and since I had successfully fulfilled all my graduation requirements, I was done with classes a full semester early. My life still centered on Wooster, and I was "allowed" to continue to live on campus until the official end of the year, a registered student but with no classes (maybe one class? I can't remember). I do remember it was a great senior spring! As the weather warmed, the blossoms bloomed, my whole future seemed ahead of me, in full.

At some point in the winter or spring I was nominated to be considered for a Rhodes Scholarship, an unimaginable honor. I flew to Tennessee to do the interviews (candidates are screened by home state), and was thrilled with the idea I was even being considered. Only one thing—my commitment to football, and the now more imaginable but still long-shot dream of playing in the NFL. Ultimately, the Rhodes committee asked me the big question—if I had to choose between the Rhodes Scholarship and a shot at the NFL, which would I choose? I answered candidly—I had too much time, sweat, blood, and tears invested in my football life to give that up without taking my shot. I don't know if that was the dispositive reason, but they chose another candidate. I was flattered to have been considered, but I never looked back.

With my college curriculum wrapped up, I found a job to make some money and keep me busy. I became a shipping guy at the Wooster Brush Company, a Wooster institution on the south side of town. The Wooster Brush Company was, at the time, the second-largest paint brush company in the world, and paint brushes, rollers, tape, all manner of painting supplies (not paint) were made and shipped out of the big facility there in Wooster. My job was to take the orders, big and small, and pack all the little stuff into shippable boxes, tape them up, and get them ready to either UPS out or load up on a large freight truck. The filled orders would roll at us all day, and we'd arrange and pack and tape as fast as we could.

My foreman on the dock was named Dick Tracy—yes, really. I think the others working there were a little skeptical that some college guy would actually work hard at this job, probably thinking that I thought it was somehow "beneath me." But I never felt that way—about this or any other job I had. And as you've seen, I have had many unglamorous jobs. I've always respected the many people I worked alongside in those jobs, for they would get up every day and go in and do it again, the same tough jobs. I felt fortunate to have the work, and even though I knew it was temporary, I wanted to be my best and show them the college boy could do an honest day's work too.

When I got there on the shipping bay, they were consistently running behind 1–2 weeks. Dick Tracy and the team couldn't ever seem to get caught up. So it was with a little satisfaction later that summer that Dick announced to our crew that for the first time in a long time, we were actually caught up. Yeah, I could pack paint brushes, all right!

Dick and the rest of the crew, of course, also knew that I was a football player, with hopes of playing in the NFL. I had been in the paper a few times (usually courtesy of Ernie Infield), and was something of a local star in Wooster. They all knew I'd been scouted, was working hard, and had some chance of being drafted. No one from Wooster had ever been drafted before, or played, in the modern NFL. As Draft Day approached, they shared my excitement with me, as did, of course, my friends, family, and Cindy. But really, I don't think many of my friends or family gave me much of a shot—what were the odds?

Draft days were April 29–30, 1980. There were 12 rounds in the draft in those days, and about 330 players were taken by the 28 teams, in reverse order of the prior season's standings. The draft was not nearly as public then as now, though it was the first draft televised by ESPN—probably watched by 10 people. Very little "draft analysis" other than what the NFL teams did themselves. And what they did themselves they tried to do secretly so as not to reveal what they were thinking or who they wanted to draft.

In those days, veteran player movement among teams was almost nonexistent because of the rules surrounding players and team rights (no "free agency" in those days). In summary, the player had few rights, the team had many. Players were "owned" by a team until the team fired them. If a player's contract expired, all the team had to do was tender a minimal offer and any other team interested had to "compensate" the other team with high draft picks/cash if it wanted the player. As a result, very few high-caliber players changed teams, and those who did usually were at the end of their careers, had an injury issue, or some other flaw. Thus, the draft was the most important way for every NFL team to obtain new talent. Do a good job in the draft, build a good team. Do a bad job—you didn't win.

With 12 rounds and over 300 players, once the draft was done the common thinking was that all the top talent, NFL-level talent, was taken. If a player wasn't drafted, even from a big university, odds were that player's football days were over. With 28 teams, there were 1,260 active roster spots in the NFL. The average career in the NFL in those days (and interestingly, today, still) was just under four years. That implies a turnover rate of almost 25 percent every year, which, of

course, varied by team. Usually poor teams had a higher turnover because they were cutting players and looking for better ones. Common
wisdom around the draft then was that if you were drafted on the first
day of the draft (generally rounds 1–5), you had a good shot to make
the team. If on Day 2, your odds at making the team were slim. And if
you weren't drafted *at all*, your odds of being invited to an NFL camp,
given a chance at making the team, and actually making the team?
Well, your odds were slim to none, and slim was leaving town.

On April 29 I worked my usual day shift at Wooster Brush while
the draft was taking place in New York City. I didn't expect to be
drafted on the first day, really, but that didn't mean I didn't harbor
some secret hope that it would happen. And the day ended without
my name being called. The first guy taken in the draft was Billy Sims,
by Detroit, who was a great running back. Cincinnati picked third
and took Anthony Munoz, an offensive tackle from USC. I finished up
my shift at Wooster Brush and went for a hard workout. I hadn't really
expected to be called that first day anyway. My day would be Day 2!

I showed up on Day 2 of the draft, April 30, with quite a bit more
anticipation. Surely this would be the day. I'd been scouted. I had
teams expressing interest in me. And I hoped one would use a late-
round pick on the center from Wooster. The draft started in the morning, about the same time as my shift at Wooster Brush. Dick Tracy and
the rest of the shipping crew were pulling for me, all hoping the call
would come through (interested teams had my work number at the
Wooster Brush shipping dock). The day seemed to drag on forever,
with no calls. Finally, the Pittsburgh Steelers, who had won the prior
Super Bowl and picked last in the 1980 draft, announced the final
pick of the draft—Tyrone McGriff, guard, from Florida A&M, unofficially labeled "Mr. Irrelevant" as the last player taken in the draft.
What did that make me? Less than irrelevant—it made me undrafted.
Slim had just left town.

However, shortly after the draft ended and we were wrapping up
our shift in the warehouse, Dick Tracy got on the speaker and told me
I had a call in the office. With some nervous excitement, I picked up

the phone. The Bengals were on the line, and they wanted to sign me as a free agent and give me a shot to make the team. Even though I wasn't drafted, the Bengals (and other teams) would try to sign a number of free agents this way, right after the draft.

With 45 players coming back from the previous year, plus 12 draftees, and maybe 3–5 injured players coming back, each NFL team wanted to do two things. First, after combing through any undrafted players, teams tried to sign any hidden gems that other teams had missed, who might have fallen through the screening process. With 12 rounds of the draft and dozens of scouts examining players on film and in person for months, there were not too many of these. The other reason, quite simply, was numbers. NFL teams liked to take about 80–90 players into training camp so they'd have enough players for drills and scrimmages and substitutes during the rigors of training camp. Basically, they needed a number of players to be there to fill out the training camp roster, take a beating, and disappear when final cuts came around.

While I thought of myself as being asked to sign for the first reason, as a "hidden gem", I'm sure the Bengals offered me a contract for reason number two—they needed another body on the field in August. I think there was also a third reason in my case, and it went back to that day in 1979 when Ernie Infield told Paul Brown they should keep an eye on me. I think Paul had a sparkle in his eye when they decided to offer the kid from the College of Wooster a shot.

Later that day I also had a call from the Cleveland Browns. They too were prepared to offer me a contract. That was certainly a compliment . . . and a complication. Remember, once the draft had finished and I had not been selected, by definition I was technically a "free agent"—a player who could sign with any team that wanted me. The Bengals and Browns both were offering similar contracts, with the Browns a little more signing bonus (more on the money later). I didn't have an agent—only drafted players needed agents, and I felt I should be able to "negotiate" my own contract. I talked to Ernie Infield, Pig, my line coach, some other close friends. Bengals or Browns?

The Browns were coming off a good year, in the playoffs. They had drafted a center late in the draft, plus they had a solid offensive line. The Bengals, on the other hand, were coming off a terrible season, and had just hired a new head coach and entire coaching staff. While they had drafted two offensive linemen (#1 and #4), neither was a center. I felt one of my advantages was that I'd be smarter than the average offensive lineman, and that a new coaching staff would be implementing an entirely new offense—new plays, new terminology, new blocking schemes—and it should be to my advantage, at least *mentally*, that we'd all be starting from scratch. Ernie encouraged me to select the Bengals for these reasons too, along with the intangible that Paul Brown was known for building a team of players not just based on athletic ability, but also character and heart—what drives the player.

I decided on the Bengals.

CHAPTER 5

The Cincinnati Bengals (1980–1984)

OF COURSE, IT wasn't quite that simple. The Bengals were basically inviting me to come to Cincinnati, agree on a "contract," and then try out for the team. Shortly after the excitement of the phone call, I made arrangements with the team to come to Cincinnati. I climbed into my well-used Chevy Monza (2+2) for the 3½-hour drive to the Queen City, a city I had driven *through* many times on the Chattanooga-Wooster trip, but never a city I had driven *to*. They put me up in a hotel downtown for one night—probably the nicest hotel I had ever stayed in to that point in my life. I got up the next morning nervous and unsure. My first visit was over to the team offices, right at Riverfront Stadium where the Bengals played their home games. I found my way to the offices, which were tucked under a part of the stadium seating, somewhat nondescript. First stop was to meet with Mike Brown, son of Paul, part-owner and the person in charge of day-to-day operations.

Mike was a Harvard lawyer by training, and responsible for negotiating all the player contracts, among other things. I had made a decision that I did not need an agent for two key reasons: first, I felt I was capable of negotiating my own contract, and second, given my "free agent" status, I doubted there would be very much to negotiate! Turns out I was *very* correct about the second reason. Sitting across from Mike in his big office, he slid a copy of the standard

NFL player's contract across his desk to me. It was already filled in, with my name and the contract numbers that had been offered over the phone. It was quite literally a multipage form contract, similar to what you would sign when leasing or buying a car (only here, *I* was the car!). The deal was pretty basic: $2,500 signing bonus, $2,500 roster bonus (paid *if* I made the team), and a salary of $25,000, to be paid over the course of the 16-game season (basically, $1,562.50 per game). It was a 3-year standard contract, which called for me to be paid $35,000 in year 2, and $45,000 in year 3. These were essentially the NFL league minimums, meaning they couldn't pay me any less even if they wanted to. All key terms in the contract were set already, as part of the collectively bargained agreement with the NFL Players Association, the players' union. I was about to become a "union man." There was no negotiation of the agreement or its terms. Here is our offer—do you want to sign? I told Mike I wanted to read the agreement before I signed it. He smiled a little smile (this was the man who would be negotiating with Anthony Munoz and his agent over a much-larger contract) and told me to take my time. When done and realizing to some degree what my "leverage" was, I asked for a couple minor adjustments. I also realized that the "contract" was really a one-way deal: the team would own me as a football player until *the team* decided it didn't want me anymore. And when they did decide that, they could terminate the contract, fire me, without having to honor the rest of it. In other words, even after signing a 3-year contract, the Bengals could have terminated it on my way back to Wooster, without any obligation other than paying me my signing bonus, the $2,500. The rest of the contract—void.

While Mike Brown was making the insignificant changes to the agreement that I had bargained for (great work, Blake!), I was taken down the hall to personally meet (for my second time) the legendary Paul Brown. I remember little of that meeting. He had an enormous office, a view of the stadium and field. A huge Bengal tiger rug, complete with tiger head, stared me down as I walked in and sat across from him. He remembered meeting me the prior summer in

Wilmington. I recall he welcomed me to the Bengals and told me to work hard. I remember little else, left his office, signed my contract, and became the property of the Cincinnati Bengals—happily!

Before the drive back to Wooster, I was taken over to the Bengals' practice facility across town. There I met the offensive line coach for the first time, Jim McNally, also a rookie in the NFL as a coach. He was a short, animated ball of energy, and as soon as I changed into shorts and cleats he had me on the field doing drills, footwork, and crazy duck-walks for the next hour. I met the team strength coach, Kim Wood, who gave me a binder of strength and conditioning programs to work at during the off-season. Strength coach? Never had one of those before—I had always been my own strength coach.

I left the practice facility exhausted from all the nervous and physical energy I had expended over the past 24 hours. I had a big check in my pocket ($2,500, less taxes), which was about the amount of money I would have earned working *all summer* in the pipe yard or at the brush company. I was upbeat, confident, the excitement of being in the National Football League, at least signed to a contract with a team, so my trip back to Wooster was a blur of thinking through the events of the last week, and more so, what I was going to be doing over the next weeks and months to make the team. I thought I could do it if I worked hard enough.

A few weeks after signing my contract with the Bengals, the first actual team activity was scheduled. Called "minicamp," it was basically a long weekend for all the rookie draft picks, free agents (like me), and a few veterans (who for various reasons were asked to attend, for instance, if coming off an injury). The camp was held on a Friday through Monday morning. I drove the Monza (2+2) back down to Cincinnati and stayed with all the other rookies at a hotel downtown. Each morning we would all pile onto a school bus (no kidding—a school bus) and ride the 15 minutes over to the practice facility, Spinney Field. Yes, there I was, a couple school bus seats from #1 draft pick Anthony Munoz, who, despite his big contract, got treated just like the rest of us rookies.

We bounced over to the practice fields, which were about 80 yards of grass field, 80 yards of Astroturf, a parking lot for a few dozen cars, and a low, featureless cinder block building with a corrugated steel roof. All surrounded by a tall fence topped with barbed wire, separating the facility from various industrial and commercial properties. If the wind blew from one direction in particular, we would get a metallic taste in our mouths while outside, something floating through the air. The inside of the building was no more glamorous. Rough carpet, old tile, about 50 steel cage lockers with hooks, and a large wooden storage box (lockers about 4 feet wide, 3 feet deep, 8 feet tall). Meeting rooms scattered about with windows blacked out so no light could impinge on film sessions. Group showers for about 10 people at a time, maybe five sinks, two windows and three or four bathroom stalls. And a training room with a few training tables for taping and treatment, some whirlpool tubs, and other typical training room stuff.

Down the hall was the equipment room, where all players were basically handed the standard daily issue shorts, socks, T-shirts, and jock. When I got mine and saw I had been issued a medium jock, I was naive enough to ask for an XL. The equipment manager looked at me blankly and told me *everyone* wears a medium. Dumb rookie. He was nice enough to issue me a pair of Astroturf shoes though, my first ever. I had only played on Astroturf a couple times in high school, and there we just wore our regular cleats or tennis shoes.

The first day was mainly physicals, measurements, conditioning, and strength tests. I think I ran the 40-yard dash in 5.1 or 5.2 seconds, somewhat average at the time for an offensive lineman. The standard strength test at the time was the bench press. Put 225 pounds on and try to do as many repetitions as possible. I wasn't prepared for this, as my lifting was mainly heavier weight sets and lower repetitions, trying to build power and strength. Still, every single test was measured, recorded, and competitive. All your position players and others were standing there watching you "perform" and making comments based on your performance. I did a very pedestrian 17 or 18 reps on the bench press, below desired level for a lineman. Some linemen did more, some less. It was clear to me that some players had hardly even lifted weights before—a surprise to me since almost all of them went to big "football program" schools.

Most of the practice time that weekend was a crash course on the playbook and the drills we would be doing to support the plays and techniques the coaches wanted us to use. I was introduced to Rod Horn at this minicamp, as previously described in the Preface. Third-round pick from Nebraska, and a nose tackle, he and I squared off all weekend. I got to meet all the other rookies who would be trying to make the team later in the summer. A few of us one night had the energy to take in a Cincinnati Reds baseball game. We all sweated and learned together, all us rookies, and by the end of the weekend, friendships had been established, and we left thinking we knew what to expect in the NFL. Boy, were we ever wrong!

A couple weeks later, the Bengals held their second minicamp, and this was for the full team, including veterans. Now, all 90 or so of us were in camp. Still just shorts and helmets, no real contact, but now for the first time all the rookies were getting a taste of the full speed and power of the NFL. Most of the rookies, as I've said, were from big university programs, so they were used to big-time football. The difference here, though, was that every NFL veteran was the best of the best. In college, the players from Nebraska might play against NFL-caliber talent a few times in a season. Here, now, *every* player on the field was NFL-caliber talent. At least the veterans were—the rookies still had to prove it. And me? In my college career, I had *never* played against an NFL-caliber player. The difference in size, speed, and violence was large between Alabama and the NFL; between Wooster and the NFL . . . it was immeasurable.

We ran through plays and drills all weekend. I was able to watch and work with and against players who were NFL vets, some stars, some all-pros. I saw quickly just how much I would have to elevate my physical skills, and it was a lot. Remember the strength test? We had linemen popping off 25 repetitions (or more) with 225 pounds.

They were running the 40-yard dash in under 5 seconds. They knew their positions and NFL techniques. My one advantage: I was smart enough to learn everything we had to learn, and fast. New head coach, new assistants, new playbook, meant that everyone started at about the same level on the knowledge side. I figured if I could get the mental part of the game down better than the others, I would have some leeway to catch up on the physical side—but not much leeway! My work was definitely cut out for me.

Back in Wooster, as final semester senior year came to a close, all of the seniors were preparing to move on from the familiarity of college and friends, to new jobs back home or graduate school. I happened to have the most unique postgraduate plans of the graduating class, I think. However, because the Bengals were not a sure thing, I had also continued with my law school application process. Accepted by Duke, rejected by Michigan and Stanford, I sent in all my housing and other forms and was all set to attend Duke Law School in the fall of 1980. Of course, that was my backup plan. Cindy had decided to go out on her own adventure, to teach English in Taiwan, which was at that particular time in Taiwan, in fact, a big adventure. She left for Kaohsiung shortly after graduation, with tearful good-byes, but each of us looking forward to our next chapter. Though engaged to be married, the opportunity for Cindy to work overseas was important. And I was staying at Wooster for the summer with really only one thing on my mind: training to make the team.

Shortly after graduation, Cindy was on a plane to Asia after prep time in New York. I was moved out of my small dorm room (and Cindy's room, where I really lived) into a one-room apartment with a shared bathroom in an old house just off campus, where I think I paid about $90 a month in rent. I had an old fridge, a mattress on the floor, maybe a chair, and my stereo system and clothes (i.e., jeans, T-shirts, and workout clothes). It was as minimalist a lifestyle as I had ever had. Cereal for breakfast, off to work, and straight from work every day to the Nautilus gym on the outskirts of Wooster. The Bengals strength coach had found this place for me to work out and were paying for it, so every other day I was there for heavy weight training. The other days I would go to the Wooster football field and do my running, stadium step training, and other drills. Every day, 6 days a week. Sundays off. I kept my job at Wooster Brush through the summer, wrote Cindy *many* letters, and due to the cost of calls we talked only once a week. Dinners were usually at the college cafeteria if open (all I could eat—maybe $4), or at a local burger joint when I had a 2-for-1 coupon. With this suspect diet, it was a little surprising I stayed as healthy and strong as I did, but being 22 years old and in great shape does allow you to eat just about anything (apparently!). And still working through that gallon of milk a day as my "core" diet. The college campus was virtually empty, with the occasional summer camp of kids coming through. The summer was good for focus, and there were no distractions, but it sure was lonely.

Finally, it was time to leave Wooster behind and see if I could make all the hard work pay off. My last day in Wooster I drove over to the football stadium. I sat in the bleachers and stared at the field where I had so many memories—wins, losses, mud, pain, sweat, blood, adrenaline. I walked down and felt the grass and imagined not ever playing again. I *couldn't* imagine it. I went up the Scot hill and sat on that bench, where before so many games I had sat, looked out over the field, *my* field, and prepared myself for the game. I took a deep breath, emotional. Even there and then, no game ahead, I could feel the adrenaline pulsing through me. The rest of my life ahead of me, I was as ready as I could ever be. I put Wooster in the rearview mirror, and set my sights on the NFL.

Training camp began toward the end of July. Camp was held in a tiny town near Cincinnati, in Wilmington, Ohio, where I had been once before on that trip with Ernie Infield. It was an unremarkable place from an appearance standpoint, a little town carved out of cornfields that happened to have a small college where the Bengals had been holding training camp for years. But the road to the NFL, for me, went right through Wilmington. Players arrived from all over the country. Similar to first day of college, except we'd met before in minicamps. The rookies were all nervous, though some much more confident than others. We checked into our spartan dorm rooms, two to a room, standard-issue college dorm bed (meaning not long enough for me), linoleum floors, no air-conditioning, and communal bathrooms. We were assigned a roommate, given a schedule, and were reminded never to be late. My roommate was a free agent like me, a linebacker from Boston College with an NFL dream of his own. We threw our meager belongings into the hot room and got ready for . . . well, we weren't really sure. But that didn't last long, because it soon became clear that practically every hour of the day would be scheduled for us.

It was easy to tell the veteran players from the rookies on check-in day. We rookies showed up, for the most part, in older cars, few belongings, and no idea what was going on. The vets rolled up in their nice cars, knowing what they were doing and having some idea what training camp survival was all about. The rookies had only a few clothes and our playbooks. The veterans moved in to their dorm rooms like a second home: air conditioners, fans, curtains, minifridges, stereos. Duct tape was quickly applied around their doors to keep the cool air in their rooms, while we rookies would sweat our way through the heat and humidity of a college dorm room in July/August. The vets knew each other and knew the training camp drill. But what they didn't know was training camp under Forrest Gregg.

We had to go through physicals again, and then we all did the strength and 40-yard dash test again. While my 40 time stayed about the same, I had achieved my goal on the strength test, knocking off 25 reps on the 225-pound bench press test. This was a big improvement from my first test, and this didn't go unnoticed by the strength coach and line coach. My test put me right in there with other linemen, and better than several. After the preliminaries we were all fitted with shoulder pads, pants, and all the other equipment we would need for practice.

We had team dinner, and then gathered as a full team for the first time, where Forrest Gregg addressed all of us as only he could do.

His eyes flashing, his 6 foot 5, 250-pound Hall of Fame frame still intimidating, he told us what he expected from us: hard work, discipline, respect for coaches and teammates. He told us we would all get a fair shot, that he didn't care who had been a starter or an all-pro. The only thing that mattered to Coach Gregg was performance—he didn't give a *damn* what you'd done yesterday. What were you doing *today*, *right now*? What would you bring to the team tomorrow? That is the team of 45 players he would keep. And he expected—demanded—our best. Anything less and you wouldn't be a Bengal very long. Camp would be hard, intense, and competitive. All this was clear from the first meeting. And we hadn't even had our first real practice yet. But when you are coming off a 4-12 season and have a new head coach who played for the legendary Vince Lombardi, was a Hall of Fame tackle and world champion—none of us should have been too surprised at Coach Gregg's approach.

First NFL training camp practice. No shorts-and-helmets routine, no couple of days of "getting used to practice." We put on our pads and headed out into the midmorning warm humid Wilmington air. The trainer led the team through about 10 minutes of stretching. Then, without warning, Coach Gregg initiated what would become one of the most dreaded parts of many training camp days: grass drills. He had us jog in place, yelling at us to get our knees up, all 90 of us across the field. He yelled "Front!" and all 90 of us would simultaneously hit the grass, prone on our stomachs. Almost immediately he would yell "Up!" and all 90 of us were to bounce up from the prone position to jogging in place, as quickly as possible. "Front! Up! Front! Up!" This seemed to go on forever. Guys who were slow to get up got special attention from Coach Gregg. All the casual chatter stopped. All you could hear was grunting, panting, and low cursing as we hit the ground and sprang back up. In full gear. Finally, Coach Gregg yelled "Front!" and no "Up," and we lay on our stomachs resting, thinking we were done. But after a few seconds, "Up!" and we were back in the middle of another set. A dozen or 15 more, then another brief rest, facedown in the wet grass, breathing heavily, wondering how to get up when he yelled "Up!" again. Usually at this point, Coach Gregg would tell us how lucky we were to be here, outside, getting exercise, and getting paid for it. He reminded us that most people paid good money to do this. None of us quite appreciated the humor.

"Up!" And off we were into another set. By this time, some guys were hardly able to get up. Some were throwing up. Some tried to get up, but before upright, the dreaded "Front!" would come, and they'd fall back to their stomachs. I struggled through all three sets—probably 50–60 total grass drills. I was dying, not sure how long I could go on . . . legs dead. I had trained all summer, but not for this! Finally, the final "Up!" . . . but that was followed by a lap around the field, which after the grass drills was like a marathon—players jogged, limped, straggled, staggered around the field, back to gather around Coach Gregg. He looked at us with a small grin, and told us now that "warm-ups" were over, it was time to get to work. I think that was when we all realized what training camp would be like.

For the first 10 days, the training camp routine hardly varied. Up at 7 a.m. and trudge over to breakfast (required) to eat something early enough to hold it down for 9:30 a.m. practice. Stumble back to the hot dorm room and lay down until 8:00 or so. Head over to the locker room and start to get ready for 9:30 practice. This included getting in line for mandatory ankle taping, an assembly-line process where some 180 ankles were taped to (theoretically) help prevent ankle sprains. I quickly learned to shave my ankles to mid-calf, to avoid the post-practice pain of ripping the tape off . . . along with hair. (I had never regularly taped up anything at Wooster, except an occasional ankle sprain or wrist.) Then would begin the methodical dressing in full equipment (cleats, socks, knee and thigh pads, hip pads, shoulder pads, helmet). You learned to leave the shoulder pads off until the last possible minute, lounging in the limited shade until warm-ups began at 9:30. Usually 75 or 80 degrees and *humid* by then, dew coating the grass and starting to steam off. Stretching and warm-ups. The dreaded grass drills—how many today? Seemed to depend on Coach

Gregg's mood and our previous practice, but usually 40–50 total. The slow lap around the field, sweating and panting.

We'd then split into position groups (offensive lineman, linebackers, receivers, etc.) and work on individual position drills with our respective coaches. This involved rapid repetition of various blocking skills and techniques, working against one of our fellow linemen. It could also involve sled work, where we took our stance and in ones or twos drove a large sled a few yards, often with our animated line coach standing on the sled urging us on. A couple of times Anthony Munoz and another lineman would lift the sled and practically throw the coach off—he learned to hold on tight.

Coach Gregg, former offensive lineman himself, would often drop over during our line drills and offer his encouragement. After line drills, we'd get together with the defensive line and linebackers and work "live" (meaning full speed and full contact) on our run and pass blocking, and, of course, the defensive line was working on their own techniques. With two centers in camp (Blair Bush, the starter, and me, the rookie free agent), we got plenty of repetitions. And since one of us was often called over to snap to the quarterbacks as they drilled, a break for *that* center, that left the other to take just about every snap with the line drills. Snap—fire out—block with head, shoulders, and arms, drive to the whistle, do it again. Or we'd line up for pass protection drills, as the defensive line practiced their rush techniques against our protection techniques. Again—snap, set up for protection, head butt and arm jam the rushers, until the whistle blew. Oh, and every single snap, every play, every block, was filmed by a camera up above. It came to be known as the "eye in the sky." This meant that almost all of practice was filmed and later scrutinized in slow motion at team meetings. In other words, every single play, every practice . . . counted. I had never had this kind of pressure before, and it basically meant I had to try to maintain a game-type level of intensity through every practice, every drill. I knew my margin of error, unlike a proven veteran or highly drafted rookie, was very low. I'd be one of the first cuts if I gave the coaches any reason to cut me.

After our position and line drills, we'd get together as full offensive and defensive squads and run a series of plays that we were working on that day. For example, we might be working on a running play off tackle, and we'd line up and run it, full speed, full contact, against our defense. The only limitation on contact was hitting the quarterback and cut blocking (blocking at the knees). Otherwise, it was full-on live. We'd then mix in passing plays and usually wrap up practice with a series of conditioning sprints— 40 yards at three-fourths speed in full gear. After a quick team meeting on the field, the special teams units (kicking, punting, long snappers, holders) would stay out and work on their specialties for 15–30 minutes. That meant I was out too, because I was one of two long-snappers in camp; Blair Bush, the other center, being the other.

The first time I watched Bush long-snap was an eye-opener. He was so fast and precise with his snaps that mine looked a full degree of separation away. Sure, I could generally snap it to the punter or holder with a good spiral and pretty good speed. But Bush sent a tight spiral back every time, to the same spot, with high velocity. On field goal snaps, he was often so accurate that the laces of the ball would hit the holder in the same place on his hand every snap—something that increased the accuracy of the field goal kicker. It made me feel like my skills were mediocre, and so after every practice I'd stay out a little longer and work on my own snapping until, while I wasn't as good as Bush, I was snapping the ball at an acceptable NFL level. How did I know? We had a special teams coach who was ex-military and who was incredibly meticulous. He had a stopwatch with him at every practice, and he timed *every* long snap. He knew to the tenth of a second how long the punt snap should take to hit the punter's hands (1.2 seconds OK, 1 second or less better) or the kneeling kick holder (.7 seconds or the kick would likely be blocked). He had that stopwatch on me all the time, working with me to help me get better. Because, you see, though I wasn't as good at it as Bush, I was the only other player in camp who could do it. The coach tried to get other players to learn to do it, but they made *me* look good, and so all those years of long snapping, the winter work in the dormitories, the after-practice sessions—all meant I had a valuable skill there in training camp.

Morning practice and "after practice" would generally wrap up around 11:45, leaving time to cut the tape off my ankles, strip off my sweat-soaked *everything*, hang it around my old metal locker, quickly shower, and get over for lunch. Now, generally at each practice I was sweating off 5–10 pounds, and for me, one issue was keeping my weight *on* (many players had the opposite issue). But usually at lunch I was so tired, and with the afternoon practice just a couple hours away, it was hard to eat. I consumed massive amounts of fluids at lunch (no milk), and some food I felt I could keep down knowing what was coming in the afternoon. We'd usually have a 1-hour rest after lunch, then walk over in the heat of the day (now usually 85–90 degrees and humid) to get ready for 3:00 practice. Get taped for the second time that day, pull on the still-wet pants and jersey (the only fresh clothes we had for each practice—socks, jock, shorts, T-shirt), and stagger out into the heat.

The afternoon ritual began with a mandatory trip to the dip bar— two metal poles suspended off the ground like parallel bars, where we were to do a set of dips (lowering and raising our body), and then jog a lap to warm-up. No grass drills in the afternoon, thank God! It was interesting to watch. This was 1980, and it is safe to say that some players still did not use weight-training regularly, or really do much off-season training at all. That changed over the years I was playing, so players seemed to take year-round conditioning more seriously. But at the dip bar, there were some players who couldn't do even one dip, including offensive linemen. And many players had real trouble making it through conditioning drills. Again, the discipline I had to get ready for camp was paying off in little ways, and I have to think coaches noticed this stuff.

We sweated and pounded our way through a typical afternoon practice session, which, in some ways, was tougher because it was the second practice of the day, and it was hotter. But I also knew that if I got through this practice, I'd made it through another day and had over 12 hours before the next 2-hour session of abuse. When I went in after the second practice of the day, it was often hard to shower I was so tired. I was usually down about 10 pounds after this practice and completely beaten up. The first week, I think every part of my body was bruised, bent, or hurt. I had a large raw spot in the middle of my forehead from using that part of my helmet as a battering ram 3–4 hours a day. My fingers were bent and jammed, legs wobbly. I was so tired. We were due at dinner at 6, where I would literally try to take in most of my calories for the day, because I wasn't in danger of puking it up on the field. I ate as much as I could, drank at least half a gallon of milk, and gorged myself on fat and calories. From there we'd be due in team and position meetings at 7:00, and those would go until about 10:00. And those sessions were intense. As I said, everything we'd done in practice was replayed, in slow motion, there in front of your teammates, with the coach critiquing every move and step. Every time I was up I could feel myself tense up, wondering . . . *How did I do on that play? Did I measure up? Was it good or bad? Would the coach mock me or compliment me?* These sessions were not for the timid or sensitive. It got to the point where I could almost recall every play of the day, so I knew whether I had a good or bad one coming up. Our line coach was so obsessive about filming that he even filmed our practice drills—to examine our footwork and technique. Exhausted after the day, and then the night film sessions, I'd fall asleep as soon as I could. There was a lights-out curfew at 11 p.m., but that was never an issue for me.

At 7 a.m. the next day, it would start again. Those first 10 days of two-a-days, with no breaks, no relief, no change of schedule, were probably the hardest 10 days of my life. Some days I wondered how I'd make myself pull on my pads again, how I'd get myself up enough to go play yet again against Rod Horn, or the other defensive linemen. It was, in many ways, pure survival. Get up, gear up, and make it through another day. Ignore the pain, deny the fatigue, get through another set of drills and meetings. Fall into my too-short, too-hot dorm room bed. Get up, do it all again. Could I do it? I refused to let myself consider quitting. One practice, one day at a time.

Of course, the veterans all hated training camp too. And so they looked for ways to make things more entertaining, which I have to say was pretty challenging in Wilmington, Ohio. It was an hour from Cincinnati and any form of entertainment a male in his 20s might be interested in. And there was that whole curfew thing (11 p.m., every night we were in Wilmington). So, in reality, all of us were essentially prisoners there on the Wilmington campus during training camp. The veterans, in a strained effort to get some form of levity during the dog days of camp, had a tradition where at lunch or dinner—usually dinner—the veterans in the lunch room, at any given moment, could "request" (translation: require) a command performance from any rookie who happened to be dining at the time. This meant that at most meals for the first couple of weeks, one or two rookies would get the call, have to stand up, and sing their school fight song or some other tune. Some of our rookies were pretty creative and good when called on. But most, like me, dreaded the call. Already tired and completely stressed from practice, now, even at mealtime there was no relaxing. I got called on only twice (being a free agent rookie no one expected to make the team had its benefits), once doing a poor and abbreviated version of the Wooster fight song "Hail to the Black and Gold," which I half-muttered in a monotone. The next time I was a bit more prepared and chose "The Frito Bandito" (aye yiyiyi—I am the Frito bandito, etc.), using our starting guard Max Montoya as my foil, ribbing him with the song, much to the delight of the *other* veterans at dinner. Not so much Max, though ultimately he had a good sense of humor so no harm done. A bit of a risk on my part, but I felt I had to show some confidence even with this little game.

The other big entertainment event during training camp was the traditional rookie talent show. Less about talent, more about vulgar, gross, and pretty damn funny humiliation of players and coaches, it was the one evening where the rookies could step out of our lower-class role and poke fun at *any* person on the team, player or coach.

The coaches and veterans were well-roasted, and, of course, the most robust roasting was reserved for Coach Gregg, whose mannerisms and lectures and intensity provided ample material. In our skit, he was portrayed by one of our offensive linemen, and he was called "the man with the laser-beam eyes," picking up on his killer stare down if you got on his bad side. This skit happened toward the end of training camp, so we'd all had some time to get to know one another, and it was a good way to blow off some steam.

Numbers. I should talk a bit about numbers. I noted that in training camp, the Bengals brought in about 90 total players. Final cut number for each NFL team was 45 players, and there were "normal" numbers of position players that most NFL teams would carry, with little room for flexibility. Examples: Most teams carried three quarterbacks, with the starter and his backup getting most of the practice time so that both could play in a game. Given the realities of injury in the NFL, at any position, the first backup had to be ready at all times. For my position, center, most teams would carry two, and a total of eight offensive linemen: five starters (center, two guards, two tackles) and three backups. The backups generally had to be able to play multiple positions on the offensive line, so though my primary position was center, as camp progressed, I could expect to see action at guard and tackle (positions I hadn't played in years). When we started camp in Wilmington, I walked into the offensive line meeting room and reality hit me right in the face. In the room, 15 players, 15 offensive linemen: five starters from last year (including starting center Blair Bush), first-round choice Anthony Munoz (he was going to make the team), fourth-round choice Billy Glass, and then the rest of us—free agents and the veteran backups from the year before. Fifteen offensive linemen. Eight spots on the roster, eight jobs. In 5 weeks, seven players would be gone—cut (most likely), traded (unlikely), or injured reserve (unfortunate). My sole focus: be one of those eight, whatever it took. Make myself valuable enough, good enough, skilled enough, to be one of the eight.

Training camp wasn't just physically stressful. The mental and psychological stress was equally tough, maybe worse. I often refer to it as the loneliest 5 weeks of my life: fiancé in Taiwan (one call per week, Sunday mornings from a pay phone in the Wilmington dorm pay phone booth). No real "friends," because the guys I was spending most of my time with—the offensive line—were the same guys I was trying to beat out for a spot on the team. Tough to get too close to guys you are trying to outperform so they get cut. And on the other side of the ball, the defensive players—well, we spent hours every day beating each other up. The coaches were on us through every practice and film session, so I could feel the knot of tension through every meeting. How was my footwork? Did I block the right guy? A good block or bad one? Or the replays of mistakes I *knew* were coming—bad snaps, penalty, missed assignments—I just waited for my name to be called and get my ass-chewing.

And all this was going on in an atmosphere where *all* the players knew that the original cast of 90 players would, in 5 weeks, be 45. Every week, a few more players were cut, the ranks were thinned of the weak, the hurt, the mentally slow, those who couldn't take it. The method for getting cut was as cold and lonely as any other part of training camp. Each morning, but especially the Monday or Tuesday after a Saturday preseason game, the cuts could be made. The head scout, who had scouted me in Wooster, had perhaps the worst job in camp. For he was also the dreaded "Turk," the guy who would make the rounds on cut day through the dorm halls at Wilmington with his list. It would usually happen early, around breakfast time. A rap on the dorm room door, the Turk there in the hall, saying to the player, "Coach Gregg wants to see you—bring your playbook." Every player knew what that meant—your time as a Bengal, and probably as an NFL player . . . was over. You were being cut, waived, fired.

My roommate, a linebacker, didn't even make it to the first preseason game. I went to breakfast after about two weeks of camp, and when I got back he was packing up his meager belongings, and then sitting on the dorm bed, blank look on his face. The Turk had gotten him. A knock, bring your playbook, and my roommate's NFL dream ended. We said some awkward good-byes, and then I left him there. When I got back from practice, he was gone, and it was just me in my dorm room. After that, I knew that any morning knock on *my* door would be for me.

Let me talk some other numbers. Recall I'd signed a "contract" with the Bengals as follows: $2,500 signing bonus (already received), $2,500 roster bonus (only collect that if I was on the opening day roster—one of the 45), and $25,000 salary. The salary only was paid, again, if I made the team. During training camp, all players were paid the same weekly pay, as part of the owners-players collective bargaining agreement. Yes, I was now a union man! Each week, in addition to room, board, and "free exercise," we were paid about $500. Doesn't sound like much, but for me, it was double what I made working other summer jobs, so I wasn't complaining. But it was also the hardest I'd ever worked for $500 a week.

Paul Brown, owner of the Bengals, , took a highly personal interest in the team and players when I was a Bengal. He actually would move into Wilmington and live there during training camp, in the dorms, so he could be around for all the practices. He didn't say much, but he was there, observing and taking things in. Paul Brown, or "Coach Brown" as we players called him, was a legend in the NFL, and in Ohio, mainly as a coach. He had earned his legendary status through years of coaching very successful teams. So the field, the players, the team, the action—it was in his blood. Coach Brown was also a gentleman and an NFL executive with perspective, which he tried to share with players who would listen.

While he was still taking an active role with the team, while I was there, he held a meeting at training camp with all the rookies where he would talk about the NFL, football, and life more broadly. He said something in my rookie meeting that I would never forget. He told us all that the NFL life as a player was fleeting, at best. We should use our time in the NFL as a *means to an end, not as an end in itself.* In other words, there would be much more to life after football, so use this NFL experience to get ready for the rest of our lives. I took that to heart and never forgot it. I wonder how many other 20-something-year-olds did the same. I think very few. The siren song of the NFL keeps players from thinking of its brevity, its transient nature; instead, while in that moment, players think of it as "normal." The NFL life, and the money, was anything *but* normal.

Now, in my own case, with my background, and comparing my physical football skills and contract to those around me—I took what Paul Brown said to heart. I would give everything I could to be an NFL player, but I would know, all along, that for me, any NFL time would merely be a short chapter in the rest of my life. Of course, the real question I cared about at the time, July1980, in Wilmington, was *how* short.

Somehow we made it through 10 straight days of two-a-day, full-contact days. The first scheduled "break" in the routine was an intra-squad scrimmage, to be held on a Saturday morning. Scrimmage maybe, but with simulated game conditions, referees, and no holding back. Those defensive guys we'd been working against the last 20 practices—now we were going after them. And they us. For us rookies, it was really a game—first chance to show under high-stress conditions what we could do. All on film, of course, and with a crowd in the high school-style bleachers of a few hundred interested Bengals fans who'd made the one hour drive up to see just what new coach Forrest Gregg was doing with their Bengals.

As one of only two centers, I knew I'd get plenty of repetitions, though mostly with the second unit and against the first-team defense. But it was great to have a break in the dreaded daily routine and actually go out and do something other than run drills and practice. I remember only that I held my own, with some good plays here and there, no real blown assignments. And for me that was huge—I had to be on my game every play, not give the coaches any reason to cut me. Had to show I was getting better, understanding the system. I felt OK after the scrimmage was over. Tired, beat up, but OK—after 20 practices and the scrimmage, I knew I could hold my own. Whether or not that meant a spot on the team remained to be seen.

We had our first time off since the beginning of training camp after the scrimmage. Twenty-four hours off. Most of the vets took off to their homes in Cincinnati. Many rookies too. But a few of us had nowhere to go, so we tried to recover by just lying around a quiet, almost deserted Wilmington College. I ate and drank and tried to get my body to recuperate, both in terms of weight and energy. Most of the muscle soreness was gone after the first seven days or so of practice, replaced with fatigue, sprained joints, and bruises. And that damn lump in the middle of my forehead, from smashing my head/helmet on my opponent on every play, was slowly getting better, or at least numb.

I made a call Sunday morning to Taiwan to talk to Cindy from a pay phone in an empty dormitory hallway. We talked for a short while, never enough, both lonely. She was one of maybe two blond Americans in a Taiwanese city of a million who spoke no English. I was one of 90 guys fighting for a job, in a strange place, full of pressure, pain, and fatigue. After hanging up, I tried to relax and enjoy that Sunday until dinner, our free time. I read, napped, ate, and just lay in my room, recovering. I also knew that night, after dinner, would be a team film session where we would all watch the scrimmage together, with full critique from the coaches, especially Coach Gregg.

I started getting nervous about that well before dinner, because you never knew exactly how you had performed, especially when it was run in slow motion multiple times. After dinner, we gathered in the main meeting room for the group session. There was a lot of nervous banter, joking, and anticipation. Coach Gregg went through the roll call, as he did before every team meeting, calling out names and confirming all were present and accounted for. One minute late for a meeting, and it cost you $50, but even worse than that was the stare down from Coach Gregg. I learned to go on "Forest Gregg" time, and set my clocks and watches and mental time 5 minutes fast (and still do to this day)—never wanted to be late.

We settled into the darkened room for the film session, run on a projector, Coach Gregg with the "clicker," which ran the film forward or backward, and in slow motion, so he and the coaches could critique every move, step, and block. Whenever I was up, in for a play, I would tense up, hoping I had managed to execute good technique, make my block, or hold the pass-rusher out. Sometimes I'd have a really good block or wheel on a rushing defender and knock him to the ground, earning the praise of the coaches. Other times I'd miss a block, or simply get beaten on the play, and I'd freeze in my seat at the criticism until we blessedly moved the film to the next play. Film sessions were exhausting for the entire room. Exactly the way Coach Gregg wanted it. He wanted every player to know every play mattered. To know he was watching and expected results. No such thing as a play off, in practice or in a game. We were expected to be on, and good, every practice and every play. After the team film session, we'd break into position groups (offensive line, defensive line, etc.) and review more film, and also start working on the next day's practice assignments. This week was different, for at the end of the week was our first preseason game against another team and players, live conditions, on TV!

The Monday after the scrimmage was a tough day for several players. As noted before, my roommate and several other players were visited by the Turk, their brief careers in the NFL over before they started. The team was cut down to the maximum number allowed (by the NFL rules) to go to the first preseason game. I think we still had our whole contingent of offensive linemen, all 15. We practiced pretty much as usual all weeklong. Two practices a day, no real breaks. Coach Gregg viewed the preseason games as just another practice, and we didn't do a lot of special study or preparation for the Denver Broncos.

The week of practice before our first preseason game finally wrapped up on Friday morning. We were briefed on travel arrangements. We'd be flying out on a chartered flight from Cincinnati on Friday afternoon, spending one night in a hotel (hotel! a glorious hotel, with air-conditioning, a real bathroom—no stalls!—a color TV—no dorm food), meet and play Saturday evening, and fly back late

Saturday/early Sunday after the game, arriving back in Cincinnati in the wee hours of Sunday morning. Oh, and one more thing—Coach Gregg required all players to wear a coat and tie on road trips. *Huh?* I don't know when I last had a coat and tie on, or when I last had one that would fit my now very large frame. I think the last sport coat I had was some brown corduroy model with patches on the elbows, from the mid-'70s. After some fast research, I was told there was a big and tall men's store off the freeway on the way to the Cincinnati airport, where I found a 52XL blue blazer, a shirt that sort of fit, a tie, and some pants. Then on to the airport in the Monza (2+2), to board our fabulous charter flight to Denver.

Or not so fabulous. As it turned out, the owners, coaches, and VIPs sat up front in the plane, in first class. The players all sat back in coach—and you can imagine how well a group of NFL-size players fit in the coach seats. Here I discovered another rookie rite. Because the team was still large in numbers, only veterans were entitled to sit two in a three-seat coach row, middle seat empty. Now, foolishly, I had decided to sit with a couple of rookies who were getting to be friends, Billy Glass (6 foot 4, 260 pounds) and the aforementioned 270-pound Rod Horn (hey, when a guy spends as much quality time beating me about the head and shoulders—you *got* to be friends). So there the three of us were, about 800 pounds of linemen, squeezed into three coach seats. We could hardly move. When the meal was served on the plane, we had to take turns eating because only one of us could move our arms at once, we were jammed so tightly together.

We arrived at the Denver airport, where we transferred to a couple of buses for the trip to the hotel—usually a Marriott. Bengals must have had a deal with the Marriott—it's where we stayed in most cities. I didn't care—it was such luxury compared to my dorm room.

Saturday, game day. It may have been a preseason game, but for me, it was the most important game of my career, of my life. For the first time I'd get a chance to play against someone other than my own teammates. How would I do? How much would I play, and when? Would I be facing their starting nose tackle or a backup? Oh, and in case I hadn't mentioned it before, I had never been to an NFL game before—*never*, not even as a spectator. My first trip inside an NFL game-day stadium would be as a player.

We had prep meetings throughout the day at the hotel, reviewing blocking assignments, plays, and the Bronco personnel. More film, of course (we could never watch enough film . . .). Pre-game meals at the time, about 3 hours before game time, were a choice of the traditional (and now, as we know, awful-as-a-pre-game-meal) steak and potatoes, or for the enlightened, pancakes (carbohydrates, easy to digest). I was so nervous it was hard to eat anything, but I forced myself because I knew the next meal was 6–7 hours away, and I needed some energy to play on. We bused over to the stadium, where the field lights were already on for our night game. We crammed into the visitors' locker room, where, again, we rookies had to double up on lockers because they were built for 45 players, not the preseason travel team. Tape, pads, cleats, last-minute review of plays. Special teams players headed out first, for early warm-up: kickers, punters, long snappers. That was me. Out the door and onto an actual NFL field, under the lights. I looked around for a moment, taking it all in. I was really there.

We warmed-up as the stadium filled in. Soon, the rest of our team came out to join the warm-ups. We stretched and ran through drills and plays, working up a good pre-game sweat. I wondered if the "mile high" altitude would bother me, but I think I had so much adrenaline pumping I could have been playing 3 miles up and not noticed. After warming up we left the field and headed back into our locker room for last-minute preparations and Coach Gregg's pre-game speech. He talked about the hard work in training camp and the opportunity to play against another team, and told us to play our hardest, even though it was "only" a preseason game. For the Bengals, it was the start of a new era, the Coach Gregg era, and he wanted his stamp on it. He called the team together, and with appropriate yells of encouragement, we streamed out onto the field.

Now, the stadium was nearly full, even for a preseason game.

The Broncos were (and are) known for their passionate fans, and here they were, maybe 60,000 of them. More fans than I had played before, perhaps, in my *cumulative* football career. And yeah, we were on regional TV. As my eyes and ears adjusted to the light and noise, I realized the noise included jeers and curses directed our way (hey—we didn't have that behavior at Wooster!). Other things directed our way included coins and batteries—where the hell was security? One hefty Bronco's fan paraded around the lower bleachers in a large barrel with straps over his shoulders—and apparently nothing else on. Straps, please hold!

The game itself was a blur. Everything went so fast. I wasn't sure when I would get to play, but expected to play. Standing on the sidelines, watching the speed and violence of an actual game, I ratcheted myself up to another level. At halftime, we all crammed back into the locker room. Here, my line coach told me I'd be playing the second half at center. The first-team starters were done, time to see what the backups could do. Back on the field, I was just telling myself to remember the snap count, make the snap, and try to at least make contact with the guy I was supposed to block. Despite all the noise in the stadium, it was amazingly quiet in the middle of the field as I called for my first huddle. The team gathered around me, the QB called the play, we broke the huddle, ran the play. Next huddle, next play. I knew what I was doing, I was making my assignments, was blocking my man pretty well. I didn't care if he was a starter (he wasn't) or a backup like me (he was)—he was mine to block, and I was getting it done. No major mistakes, and I felt pretty good overall about the half I had played. I was too pumped up to get tired and couldn't believe it when the game was over. I was so excited I didn't sleep all the way home, arriving at the Cincinnati airport (which, by the way, is in Kentucky) in the early-morning hours. I didn't really wind down until I got back "home" to my dorm room at Wilmington College, where I lay down, knowing I'd made it through my first preseason game, and pretty well. I had a whole Sunday until dinner to relax, and finally fell asleep.

I was up the next morning, late, to make my weekly call to Cindy halfway around the world. Told her about my game, and now only three weeks to go in training camp and decision time—would I be on the team or not? Cindy was growing weary of her time in Taiwan and talked of coming home early if I made the team—if I had a job. More incentive. During that lazy Sunday there were only a few of us rookies around, and we were mostly sleeping and recovering from the trip. And also getting ready for that night's meetings and film session, hosted by our own Coach Gregg. First game film. And more mandatory NFL cut-downs on team size Monday. For me that meant two things. First, would I survive the cut? Second, if I did, would all those *other* offensive linemen, centers, cut by other teams, be deemed better than me? Would the Bengals sign one of those new free agents . . . and then cut me? The competitive meat grinder chewed on.

Monday morning came and went. No knock on my door. I went out to practice; several of my now former teammates did not. We started a new week of practice, twice a day, full pads, hot sun, grass drills. After the first preseason game I knew I could play in the NFL— but would I be able to hold my spot for the next three weeks?

Training camp continued its relentless routine. Dull, painful, repetitive, smelly, sweat-soaked, exhausting. When we weren't on the field we were in meetings getting jammed with plays and blocking information. I was told to start learning other offensive line positions (guard and tackle), as our linemen ranks were being trimmed. Eventually there would be eight of us, five starters and the three backups who had to be ready to play at least one additional position.

Our time at Wilmington was so structured and disciplined that the very structure and discipline became the main form of entertainment. Who would be late for a meeting and get the Forrest Gregg Stare? Who would miss breakfast and get called out in the team meeting for doing so? Who would dare miss curfew? We never knew what one of our teammates may have done or forgotten to do, but it was part of the daily drama. Coach Gregg expected all of us to be in our seats 5 minutes *before* every meeting.

One day the coach was calling the roll and in walked a veteran player—before the technical meeting time—but barely. Coach Gregg called him out. "Where have you been—you're late!" The player, for some crazy reason, chose to argue. "I'm not late—it is *my* time until meeting time!" Oh boy. Coach Gregg replied, *"Your* time?! *Your* time?! *You* have *no* time! It is *all my time* while we are in camp, *every minute*. You are always on *my time*!" And that ended that discussion, along with a $50 fine.

Another day we were all out stretching before our afternoon practice. In an amazing show of mercy, that morning practice had been cancelled by Coach Gregg. Instead, we were all to report in for a brief weight workout with the strength coach. A wonderful change-up from the normal 2-hour pounding in the morning. Coach Gregg circled through the team, stretching and sweating on the grass. He finally found who he was looking for. "Winston! Winston!" he yelled. "Where the hell were you this morning?! I give you one break. All I ask is you show up for weight training, and you weren't there. Where the hell were you?!"

Now, Winston (as I'll call him), a big, strapping rookie defensive lineman, was fixated on the intense Coach Gregg, who was glaring down at him, repeatedly asking, "Winston—where the hell were you?!" He was nailed, caught—had nowhere to go. The whole team was silent, expectant, not sure where this would end. Finally, Coach Gregg asked him one last time—"Where the hell were you?!" Winston, screwing up all his courage, blurted out the only thing he could think of under that kind of pressure, with the eyes and ears of the entire team on him. He stammered out, "Coach . . . I . . . I . . . I was, somewhere." There was a pause. Somewhere? *Somewhere?* The laughter started slowly, and then built, rippling around through the team and broke over the practice field like a pent-up thunderstorm. Coach Gregg did all he could do to keep from bursting out laughing too. He fined Winston on the spot and told him he had to do a special makeup session in the weight room that he, Coach Gregg, would attend personally. As you can imagine, for the rest of that camp, he was "Somewhere" Winston.

Our next preseason game was a home game. First time I'd get to put on the Bengals uniform and play in front of the home crowd at Riverfront Stadium. After a lighter practice on Friday morning, that afternoon we headed down to stay at a hotel in Cincinnati the night before the game. This would be our routine for all home games—Coach Gregg wanted to know all his players were tucked into their rooms by 11 p.m. the night before the game. As the weekend before, it was just great to escape Wilmington and the cinder block dorm room. And get a break from the two-a-day practice routine.

We prepped a little more for this preseason game, both coaches and players moving closer to an actual "game week" prep routine. By the time of our final preseason game, we would be in full regular season prep mode, in terms of practices and meeting schedules. We played our second preseason game under the lights Saturday night, again the adrenaline pumping, but this time everything wasn't a "first" for me. I again got about two quarters of work in at center, and again played well enough and hit my assignments. I still played all my snaps at center, which was fine by me as that was my comfort zone and where I took almost all my practice plays. But I knew if I wanted to be one of the final eight, that at some point, I'd have to show I could play guard and/or tackle.

Under Coach Gregg, we continued with two-a-day full-contact practices right up until the final preseason game. With numbers reduced every week, that meant more repetitions in practice and more hitting. On the other hand, my mind and body had adjusted to the routine. There was practically no fat left on me. The bruises and pain points (e.g., forehead) had mostly healed—and though replaced by new ones, these were more easily ignored because of my mind-set. We linemen developed our own crude sense of humor to help us toil through the endless summer days. The banter of mutual survivors. One of our guys had a favorite line that he'd throw out before just about every practice, particularly the second practice of another hot day: "Blake, it's mind over matter—they [coaches] don't mind, and we [players] don't matter." Boy did that ever sound right.

In the third preseason game, I played more than a half, mostly at center, but also a few plays at guard. Though nervous playing guard, this was a good sign because it meant the line coach was testing me to see if I could play something other than center. Remember, the three backup linemen had to be able to play multiple positions. The Turk passed noiselessly by my door the Monday morning after. And this was a big week for another reason—the last week of training camp in Wilmington. We practiced our normal schedule that week, though again with more focus on the opponent to better simulate an actual week of real-game preparation. This involved more film of our opponent, and less time watching film of our practice drills (thank God!). This was also the week we would break camp before our last preseason game, pack up our stuff, and leave Wilmington for Cincinnati for the regular season. Of course, with the final cut coming the Monday *after* the last preseason game, for most of us rookies (those left), that meant moving into a hotel in Cincinnati to await the final roster announcement.

Coach Gregg established another new tradition in Bengals training camp, one that came with rumor and mystique until we did it for the first time: the nutcracker drill. Usually held just before we broke training camp, this was the man tester, the ultimate gladiatorial situation in football, and Coach Gregg loved it. The drill was simple. Two blocking dummies were laid parallel about six feet apart. Two players, for example a center and nose tackle, would line up across from each other between the dummies. A running back would line up directly behind the offensive lineman, prepared to take the ball from the quarterback at the snap. On the snap, the two opposing players would fire out into each other full speed, as low and hard as possible, trying to get leverage on the other. The offensive player would try to drive the defensive player out of the way. The defensive player would try to throw off the offensive player and tackle the running back, who was *required* to run between the blocking dummies. It was the ultimate in hand-to-hand, head-to-head combat. The collisions were tremendous. There was a reason it was called the nutcracker.

Now, we players, some of whom had been with Coach Gregg on other teams, had heard this drill was coming. But we didn't really know what an event it would be. The coaches the night before decided on the "pairings"—offense *vs.* defense. The entire team gathered around the drill area, yelling and pulling for their defensive or offensive teammates to drive the other guy into the ground. Coach Gregg personally ran the drill, and loved every minute of it. If the back ran outside the dummies, the drill was run again. The whole thing was, of course, filmed for future entertainment. I was nervous as hell. This was just the kind of physical, pressure-packed test that Coach Gregg wanted to see all his players endure. And I mean all—only quarterbacks and kickers were excused. Offensive linemen usually got two shots, one against a defensive lineman, one against a linebacker. When my time came, I got over the ball (as a center, we snapped the ball in the nutcracker) and screwed myself as low as I could. The only thing that mattered was hitting the guy in front of me with my face mask in his chest or neck, and driving him out of the way. The defensive lineman was doing the same, so when the quarterback called "hut," we drove into each other with a terrible collision. I couldn't get him out of the way, but did manage to deliver a good shot. More or less a stalemate. I had a better go against the linebacker, who I had 30–40 pounds on, but still it was a smacking collision. This was no time to be timid, no time for finesse. This was the brutality of football at its rawest, and Coach Gregg wanted to see how his players, in particular linemen and linebackers, responded. If you flinched in the nutcracker drill, you weren't playing for Coach Gregg very long.

The nutcracker would go on for half an hour or so, collision after collision. Tempers would flare, the occasional fight, all of which Coach Gregg viewed with a gleam in his eye. When we offensive linemen got to match up on a linebacker, that was usually good given our size advantage. Usually. There was one linebacker, a veteran named Jim LeClair, to whom the "usually" did not apply. Jim was a tough, old-school linebacker from a college in the upper Midwest, and was, by his own admission, a "farm boy." But this "farm boy" loved contact and loved the nutcracker. He would crouch down so low in his stance that there was no getting under him. He had a large, hardened pad that extended along one arm from hand to elbow, wrapped up with several rolls of tape—it looked like a small log, not an arm. And he would wind up the padded forearm and bring it crashing into your chest, throat, and head, while yelling wildly. Jim was not the linebacker you wanted to face in the nutcracker, as I learned the hard way. Coach Gregg loved him.

We went into the last week of preseason with about 60 players still on the roster. I had no idea if I was going to make it or not. And I had a big decision looming: I had to tell Duke Law School if I was coming, or if I was asking for a deferral. I screwed up my courage to go talk to Coach Gregg one morning before practice. I told him my issue, the decision I had to make, and asked if he could give me any indication of my chances, to help me decide what to do. If I deferred Duke, and didn't make the team, I was screwed, delaying my start to graduate school by a year, with no backup plan. He listened, and then told me there were no guarantees, but he liked what I'd done so far and thought my chances were good. He told me to keep working. With that somewhat positive reinforcement, after leaving his office in the Wilmington dorm, I let Duke know my decision: I was deferring. The die was cast—I either made the team . . . or not. And one of the strongest memories I have of that last week of camp was sitting in my room, alone, actually reading the want ads in Cincinnati. What would I do if I were cut? I'd have to get a job, some job, to hold me for a year to law school. There seemed to be a lot of openings for car salesmen. Was this my fate? Not if I could help it. With Coach Gregg's words etched in my mind all week, and having made it this far, I was going to finish strong, one way or the other. I had a good week of practice. My energy level was high. I knew what I was doing at center, guard, and tackle. My long-snapping skills had gotten good enough that only two of us handled this during practice and games—Bush and I. In the last preseason game, not only did I play well at center, but for a couple of series my coach put me in at tackle, just to see what I could do. Very different for me being out on the end of the line, facing the speedier defensive ends. But I knew my assignments, and my techniques we'd practiced endlessly, and did OK.

After the game, I went back to the hotel to sit out Sunday, the last day before final cuts. We all knew the coaches were huddled together trimming the roster to the final 45, each position coach laying out his case for his group of players (linemen, linebackers, receivers, etc.), subject to review and approval by Coach Gregg. The coaches' livelihoods depended on picking the right group of players. The players' NFL careers depended on the coaches' decisions. At the end of the day, as I learned later, I made the team at the expense of a 10-year veteran. My youth, ability to play multiple positions, and my long-snapping skills put me on the team. But there was no big announcement, no phone call. I found out when I drove my Monza (2+2) over to the Spinney Field practice complex Monday morning. I walked in the door and into the locker room, not knowing what to expect. The Turk was there, players were being called in and cut as they walked in the door. I caught his eye as I walked in. He let a little smile leak out on a day that had to be a tough one for him too. He didn't say anything, and I walked on past, heart pounding. The veteran starters who pretty much knew they had made the team were getting their lockers set up, stuff put away.

I made my way back to the equipment manager to get my gear and see about a locker. I half-expected him to tell me to leave, that I hadn't made the team when I asked him for my laundry and pads. Instead, I tentatively asked him if I'd made it, and he smiled and confirmed what I'd been working for those last weeks, months, years, a lifetime—had actually happened. *I'd made the team.* I was a bit in shock. I couldn't jump up and down and scream "I did it!" But that's what I wanted to do. I felt like I was walking on air. I was a Cincinnati Bengal. I was in the NFL.

I found my *pro* locker and settled in. Soon enough, we were in our first team meeting of the 45 [note: actually always more than 45 because players on injured reserve—who couldn't play for the season—were included] players who would start the season. Coach Gregg was brief in his "welcome," talking about keeping the 45 men he was ready to go to battle with. And that we had one thing only in mind—win, win, win. And we would work as hard, as long, and be tougher than any team we played. And he meant it. Coach Gregg was not a finesse guy. We would win with toughness, discipline, and hard work. Think nutcracker drill. Think grass drills. Think full-contact practices for weeks. This was a team molded in his image, one that I'm sure imitated his Vince Lombardi teams with the Green Bay Packers. And this all resonated with me, confirmed the way I'd made it here in the first place. I was all in, and bought into the program and philosophy 100 percent. And then it was time to get to work, get ready for our first regular season game just 6 days away. No time to waste.

NFL teams run on a schedule. Coaches like predictability, routine, and don't like surprises or disruptions to the schedule. Our regular season schedule was set that first week and hardly varied at all over the next 16 weeks. Monday was light work, weights, and a brief practice, treatment for injuries, and review of the prior day's game film. Usually this was a half-day session. Tough to do much more after playing the day before. Tuesday was our day off, union mandated—not sure Coach Gregg would have given us a day off if the collective bargaining agreement didn't call for it. This was a day for players to spend with families, or get personal business done. For me, my first Tuesday was finding a nondescript apartment I could afford so I could move out of the hotel (the Bengals quit covering the hotel when the season started), and so I'd have a place to live with Cindy. Yes, hallelujah, Cindy decided to come back from Taiwan when I made the team (had a job!) and live with me in Cincinnati. First home together—on Hamilton Avenue, Cincinnati, Ohio.

Wednesdays and Thursdays were our heavy workdays. Arrive at Spinney Field by 8 a.m. Team meetings (yes, still with the roll call) shortly thereafter. Some top-down info on our upcoming opponent. Then we'd break into position meetings to put in that week's game plan—which meant learning which of our running and passing plays we'd be focusing on this week, and how we would block against their defense. Scouting reports on their defensive personnel, tendencies, and film, film, film. We met nonstop until lunchtime, ate something fast (many people brought sandwiches in, like carrying a lunch pail to work—I did), then off to the training room to get taped. Usually we'd squeeze in one more meeting, and then out to practice about 2:30, full pads/full contact, where we would run through individual drills like we did in training camp, but abbreviated so we had time to put in and practice our blocking game plan. Oh, and no grass drills anymore! Those ended with training camp.

Because there were only 45 players, we would work against our own defense, mimicking the opponent of that week, and vice versa. As a backup, I got more reps with the other backups while running the "scout team," but we all did our time. I also got reps running our offense, since we all had to be ready in case anyone went down.

Practices were lively and spirited. Coach Gregg demanded full speed action and attention. If we didn't get it right, we might start the drill all over again. Every practice ended with conditioning running, usually 8–12 40-yard runs at 75 percent speed. Special teams players would stay out for skills practice (snapping, kicking), and then in the weight room for half an hour one of the two days. Usually showered and in the car at 5:30 or 6. Like a regular job, but hardly! Fridays were similar but more meeting time, and practice usually a bit shorter and in shorts and shoulder pads and helmets (we *always* had our helmets on at practice), so not a full-contact day. Fridays we'd usually put in our special situation offense (goal line/short yardage) and practice the "2-minute drill," the rapid fire, no huddle offense used just before halftime and at the end of the game. Usually wrap up by late afternoon on Fridays after another weight room session. Saturday, we'd have meetings and a no-contact practice in the morning. For home games, we'd be done at noon and have free time until checking in at the team hotel for the night at 6 p.m. or so. More meetings, then curfew at 11 p.m. If we had a road game, we'd get the morning practice in, then go straight to the airport and catch our charter flight to the opposing city, check into the hotel, same evening routine. Sunday for a 1:00 game we'd be at pre-game meal about 9 or so, perhaps followed by a meeting, and then to the stadium by 11 a.m. to get taped and ready to take the field and warm-up at noon. Game time 1–4. If a home game, we were done for the day around 5:30 by the time we were showered and out. If an away game, off to the airport and get back Sunday night whenever we got back. Pittsburgh and Cleveland, not so bad—Houston and West Coast games made for late nights. Monday—start all over again.

The final roster, the team of 45, was, I think, somewhat unique by NFL standards, certainly then and probably now. We had 45 good players, good athletes, all very highly skilled. What was unusual to me was the high overall IQ of that team, the smarts. Paul Brown was known to look for smart players—given a toss-up between two pretty equal players he would pick (or "encourage" the head coach to pick) the "smarter guy." On our 1980 Bengals team, we had players from Harvard (punter/receiver), Dartmouth (linebacker), Lehigh (receiver), and Augustana (QB). To have even one player from an Ivy League school was unusual—two was an aberration. And two players from small Division III colleges (Augustana and Wooster), one of whom was the starting QB—all in all, quite an unusual mix, I thought.

Now that's not to say we didn't run through our share of players who weren't necessarily Ivy League material. One time we were boarding the bus after a team event, late in the preseason. As was customary, Paul Brown—the owner and a coaching legend— would sit at the front of the bus and greet or nod at the players as they boarded. One of our rookies climbed on the bus, a big tight end. He paused when he passed Coach Brown's seat, looked at him, and said, "Why do people call you Coach?" Well, he was gone the next week. I already told you about "Somewhere" Winston. Then there was one of my fellow offensive linemen, we'll call him Jimbo. One day in late August or early September, we had one of those scorchingly hot days that can happen in Cincinnati. The air temp was in the high 90s, maybe touching 100. We were practicing that day on the Astroturf, a dark green synthetic plastic that soaked up the sun's heat and shoved it back at us through our face, feet, every pore on our bodies. We were all suffering through a full gear practice, not sure how we were going to make it. The rubber soles of our Astroturf cleats were starting to soften and melt.

About an hour in, right in the middle of practice, we hear Jimbo yelling out, "I can't take it anymore! I can't take it!" He fell to the ground, wrestling with his own shoes. What was he doing? Had the heat done him in? Finally he ripped his shoes off, fumbled inside them, and pulled out metal plates he'd had in there for arch support, but on this day, they were acting like a hot griddle pulling the heat from the turf right into his feet. We roared with laughter. Of course, we shouldn't have been too surprised. This was the same Jimbo who took on one of those Ohio steakhouse challenges—eat the 6-pound steak and your meal is free. You've heard of it. They also insist you eat a normal side salad and potato with it, of course, to decrease the odds of donating the meal. Well, when Jimbo sat down for his challenge, he was ordering *additional* side dishes as he ate, and he *still* finished the damn thing for his freebie. OK, then.

I've talked a little about our team, our roster makeup. I should spend a little time on Coach Gregg's rather unique relationship with our kickers, both punters and field goal kickers. His attitude toward them on a good day was tolerant. On a bad day, he wasn't sure why they were taking up a valuable roster spot, and he let them know it. When I arrived in camp, we had a veteran kicker, who for whatever reason seemed to arrive in camp on Coach Gregg's bad side. We had a mid-round draft choice in camp, providing direct competition to the vet. Whether it was money or results (results seemed about even to my untrained eye), the vet was gone before the season started, off the team but picked up by another team where he enjoyed a long and successful career. The rookie draftee never made it to the first game, unable to survive Coach Gregg's expectations (which were: kickers should make kicks—*always*. After all, that's *all* they had to do!). In came a CFL guy Coach Gregg was familiar with, but about 11 games into the season and after a 4-game losing streak, not *entirely* the kicker's fault, he was gone too. That brought back our already once-cut rookie draftee, for another shot at the big time.

We were playing in Cleveland, at the Browns (ironically, named after Paul Brown). No love lost between these two teams, especially given the manner in which the Browns and Coach Gregg had parted ways when he was fired as head coach there. Let's just say we understood it didn't sit too well with Coach Gregg. That led to his tenure in the CFL before eventually returning to the Bengals. When we got ready to play the Browns, Coach Gregg brought a special level of intensity to the week of preparation.

As we rode the team buses from the airport to our hotel in downtown Cleveland, I'll never forget Coach Gregg getting on the bus microphone and telling us all sternly that he didn't want *any* of us out alone in that city—it wouldn't be safe. Now, remember, he is talking to a busload of professional football players, most large and formidable, and he was worried any one of us might get mugged (or worse) in Cleveland!

This was a special game for me for another reason. Given its proximity to Wooster, I had a few friends in Cleveland from college days. A few of them loaded up their cars in central Ohio and after a Wooster stop came by the hotel the night before the game when I had a couple hours of free time. One of them had stuffed a Coccia House pizza (Wooster's finest) under the hood on top of the engine, so even after a one hour drive on a cold November day it was still piping hot there in the lobby of the hotel. The several of us College of Wooster grads gorged on our student staple and reminisced. I was asked a lot of questions about the NFL.

We then set out for my remaining pre-curfew time to drop by a club where an old teammate of mine had a band that was playing—Rich Sulzer, one of the biggest players in Wooster history up to that time, around 300 pounds. He was our right tackle with me for a couple years. His band was playing in what could only be described as a dive bar. I was nervous the whole time about curfew, had nothing or perhaps one beer to drink, and was glad to get back safely well before 11:00 (remember Coach Gregg's safety lecture!). For this outing I had invited our kicker and a couple other rookies to come along. We all reported back before curfew and bed check, but I am sure the others had more than one beer. I am also sure they made "friends" with some of the ladies there, as I heard well after the fact that some of them managed to restart their good times after curfew and well into the night.

Next day dawned cold and gray in Cleveland. After our normal pre-game meal and meetings, we bused over to Cleveland Municipal Stadium. Built decades ago, it was a mass of gray concrete and steel and aluminum surrounding a field that at that time of year was begging for grass. Built for both football and baseball, there was virtually no effort to grass the baseball infield, which was rough dirt and rocks. The inside of the stadium, or the visitors' locker room, made me think fondly of my old steel lockers at Wooster. Here we dressed under the unheated dripping underside of the concrete stadium bleachers, sharing lockers, and after the game, learning there was no hot water to cut the Lake Erie chill.

We took the field and played like crap. The Browns got ahead, and we couldn't seem to score. Each time we got to their end of the field, our offense bogged down. In would come the field goal unit, where I played one blocking end, since our starting center was long snapping. In came our kicker, finally making it in the NFL, his first game kick. The snap, the kick. I heard a dull thud. The crowd roared. The ball was rolling around behind the line of scrimmage until someone fell on it. Our kicker had kicked the ball into the back of one of *our* linemen, about 5 feet off the ground. He trotted over to a glaring Coach Gregg. Another time down the field, we stalled again. In we go for the field goal try. In comes our kicker. Snap, kick, thud. Unbelievable. Again into the line went the ball, and again he trotted over to a Coach Gregg who was by now apoplectic. We finished the game, took our cold showers, and left the stadium. The kicker was gone the next day, replaced by our fourth kicker in one season.

Like any job, I suppose, the NFL season can get routine for a player. We practiced and drilled every week with pretty much the same schedule, little variation. One exception Coach Gregg made was our first trip to play the Houston Oilers, in the then fairly new and still stunning Astrodome. At the time, there were still very few domed stadiums in the U.S., and this was the only one we would play in all year. Rather than our normal Saturday flight, we headed down to Houston on Friday afternoon.

The next morning we went over to the huge Astrodome for our Saturday morning practice. Coach Gregg then revealed the reason for our early arrival in the locker room before we headed out to practice. "Men," he said, "I know a lot of you, especially you rookies [he usually preceded 'rookies' with 'you' in a demeaning way, to make sure we knew who we were] have never been in the Astrodome before, and never played in a domed stadium. Now, I don't want any of you guys going out there tomorrow and getting sunburned on the roof of your mouth." Here he paused, tilted his head back, mouth gaping open, staring upward. "I don't want any of y'all staring at the dome while the game is going on, so I want *all* of you to go out there, lie on the turf, and stare all you want right now." Whereupon we all trooped out, stared at the domed roof, then practiced, and the next day, none of us were worried about looking at the Astrodome roof (which, by the way, was *amazing*!).

No, we were too busy watching Earl Campbell, who was in his prime, run over, through, and around our defense. He was a one-man attack. Hand him the ball, toss him the ball, pass him the ball. The show was on the field, and I had a close-up view. He was not tall, but his legs, his thighs, were enormous. When he leaned forward, the only thing a defender could see were his helmet, shoulder pads, and thundering thighs coming at him in a blur. On one play late in the game, which we were losing handily, Campbell broke through the line, past the linebackers, picking up speed. The only person left with any shot to tackle him was a (poor) defensive back. Campbell though was so fast that he had a choice—angle away from the defensive back and score a touchdown, or, and his mind clicked perhaps automatically to this choice—run directly *at* the defensive back. Our DB didn't have a chance. He glanced off Campbell's thighs like a dog who has, to his surprise, actually caught a car. Campbell churned into the end zone. What a display that was. Guess we should have focused more on stopping Campbell and less on the Astrodome roof.

My role on the team also settled into a relative routine. During the practice week I'd share practice snaps with our starting center as we ran through our offensive plays, though he would take a few more than I. When we were running the other team's offense for our defense, we also shared, but I took more of these snaps. I'd also rotate in for some plays at guard, and occasionally tackle, to try to develop the skills there too. I was also involved in much of the special teams in practice and in games.

As the backup long-snapper, we spent time every practice working on this in pairs, or running actual plays. On game day, I was normally in as a large blocking end on field goals and extra points, and also served time on the kick return team as part of the "wedge." Some explanation is in order on this last point. Common practice for the kick return team was the "wedge return," where two–four players would form together just in front of the receiver catching the kickoff. The wedge would gather, often grab hands, then on the "go!" yell from the receiver would start running full speed at the kickoff team players who were running full speed at us, to tackle the return man. Our job was to act as a human wedge flying as a solid 1,000-pound wall into a small area of the field, crushing and blasting any defenders who got in our way.

The defenders weren't stupid, and when they were in the path of the wedge, they did what any halfway intelligent person would do— they went low at us at our legs and knees, to break up the wedge. Perfectly legal for them to hit those of us in the wedge low, in the knees. But a recent rule change prohibited us from going low on them. So, wedge duty was strictly reserved for backups, expendables like me because of the inherent risk. This was one of the things we got paid to do.

Now, we weren't stupid, either. We learned how to anticipate the kneecap shot, so legs weren't planted. Or we went down low with them, helmet to helmet, shoulder pads to shoulder pads, low to the ground. It made for some awful collisions. Of course, if timed well and executed well, the wedge could pop open a seam in the return coverage and result in a big kick return. But not very often.

I also got occasional playing time during games if there was an injury. I stayed near the line coach most of the game on the sideline while our offense was in, taking in the game, his commentary, and being ready to go in if needed. A very unusual position for me as I had been a starter since I was a junior in high school. In some ways, I found it harder to have to be ready to go at a moment's notice, and at two or three different positions. I also got some mop-up time at the end of games if the score was lopsided one way or another. But I hadn't had a lot of steady game action. That changed on November 2.

On Sunday, November 2, our starting center hurt his thumb. Apparently it got caught and smashed between his helmet and another player's helmet or pads. Doesn't sound like much, and all NFL players, particularly linemen, played with minor-to-medium injuries all the time. It was part of the game. But this smashed thumb was on his right hand, his snapping hand, and he couldn't grip the ball and get it back to the QB with any confidence. During the practice week leading up to the game (vs. the Oakland Raiders), I took virtually all the snaps at center. Bush tried to tape up his finger, tried snapping left-handed, but it looked like the center from the College of Wooster would be getting his first NFL start. Final decision was reserved until game day, but I prepared as though I would be the starter, and I felt as ready as I could be. I knew my assignments as well as those of my other linemen. I had watched film ad nauseam on the Raider's nose guard until I knew his style and tendencies. We drilled on the Raider's pass rush over and over again, getting ready for their blitzes and line stunts. I was ready, but nervous. I'm sure my line coach was just plain nervous.

We made the cross-country flight to Oakland. By this point in the season, I had easily logged more air travel than in my prior 21 years combined. We holed up in the hotel, and I was extra focused on my playbook and being mentally prepared. Game day arrived in Oakland cool and sunny. I was wired, the adrenaline probably started at the pre-game meal. I tried to go through my usual routine, but it wasn't usual. My line coach confirmed I'd be starting, told me to be ready. My other offensive linemen offered me encouragement. We headed over to the Oakland Coliseum, home of the silver and black Raiders, Al Davis, a tradition of winning and crazy fans. Ironically, my little brother George had been a Raiders fan his entire life, and here I was playing against them.

All NFL players have pre-game routines, ways of getting their game face on. Mine remained similar to my Wooster routine: get taped, last-minute run-through of plays and drills, then find some space to block out as much as I could and get mentally prepared for the mental and physical war to come. Only now I knew my war would be in front of 70,000 fans, and a TV audience, against NFL talent. It was a long way from that bench at the College of Wooster, where I used to gaze out at the Fighting Scot field getting ready to play Muskingum, or Oberlin, or Wittenberg. A long way.

Other players tried to siphon off the pre-game energy by moving around the locker room engaged in loud banter. Others tried to find a dark corner. Some players would always use the same trainer for taping, the same sequence of getting dressed. The pregame ritual. One I'll never forget was my friend Dan Ross, or Danny Ross. He and I carpooled together to and from practice many days in Cincinnati. He was a Boston kid, blue-collar player in all the best ways, and developing into a star as our tight end. Danny's pre-game ritual was a combination of nerves and habit most likely, but everyone in our locker room knew that we couldn't take the field until the sound of Danny retching in the bathroom filtered into our space: Danny has puked—time for us to play ball!

Each game, either the offense or the defense, would be introduced player by player, before the game, and run out onto the middle of the field. As luck would have it, this week our offense was being introduced, so there I was, standing in the Oakland Coliseum tunnel with our other offensive starters, waiting for my name to be called and run out onto the field. I hoped I didn't trip and fall. My name was called out on the loudspeakers: "Blake Moore, Center, Wooster College," and filled with emotion and energy, I sprinted out into the sunlight.

The biggest game of my career had begun. It was a struggle for the Bengals. We had trouble generating a lot of offense and points. Our defense was having a tough day, and we gave up a long kickoff return for a touchdown. I focused on my nose tackle, my blocking assignments, and my line calls, the center being largely responsible for making the blocking calls.

As the game progressed, I got more comfortable, confident in what I was doing. On passing downs the Raiders would bring in four defensive linemen to rush our quarterback, and it was the job of the five offensive linemen to keep the four of them off our QB, along with the occasional blitz of an extra linebacker. One of their defensive linemen was the famous (infamous?) John Matuszak. Matuszak was quite possibly the largest human being I had ever seen. Every part of his body was huge, outsized—feet, legs, hands, arms. His head looked like it had been forced into his Raiders helmet, smashed in there with his wild hair, full beard, and snarling face. Scared the hell out of me just looking at him. On passing plays he lined up directly over my right guard. Usually I would not have a defender directly over me, so after the snap my job was to check for blitzing linebackers, and then help out one of my guards. Well, with this behemoth bull-rushing the guard into the backfield, my choice of who to help was pretty easy.

With his size, Matuszak's preferred "technique," if you can call it that, was to simply drive his 6 foot 7, 300 pounds into and over the opposing lineman, the premise being that the shortest way to the quarterback was directly through the poor guard blocking him. My guard was by no means small or weak, but Matuszak was a monster.

So, time after time, Matuszak would slam into my guard, my guard would "give ground grudgingly," and after checking my blitz pickups, I would swivel to my right and chop Matuszak down at his knees (perfectly legal at the time, but brutal). He would go down like a California redwood, and my cuts became increasingly effective as I got the hang of it. But big John only had one rushing technique. He'd line up and bull-rush again, and I'd go cut him again. Over and over. My fellow lineman was laughing back in the huddle, telling me to keep pounding him.

At some point in the second half, after yet another vicious cut block, Matuszak jumped up and towered over me, glaring down at me. "Hey, rookie—cut that shit out!" he yelled at me. I didn't know what to say—not a lot of chatter usually between linemen during a game. I resorted to "negotiation" and said something like, "Well, then, quit rushing the passer," and went back to the huddle. Yeah, that told him! My guard was chuckling, though a little concerned that I was really infuriating the giant. I didn't stop.

We battled but lost the game. My performance overall graded out pretty well. No glaring errors, blocked my assignments, and had held my own. I didn't like losing, but was satisfied with my own personal performance. After the game I heard a third-hand story that came down from the press box. One of our Bengals folks up there had apparently been near Al Davis as the starting lineups were being announced. According to the story, when I ran out on the field as the starting center, "Blake Moore, Center, Wooster College," Davis exclaimed something like "Where the hell is Wooster College, and why aren't we scouting there?" Funny stuff. I'll bet Al had never heard or said the word "Wooster" until November 9, 1980—of course, neither had most of those in the stadium or watching on TV.

The rest of my rookie season was a blur. A 16-game season, preceded by 4 pre-season games, was incredibly long, particularly when losing. We would finish the regular season 6-10 that year, a slight improvement over the previous year, but still 10 losses. I had only 14 losses in *four years* of college! And once we knew the playoffs were out of reach, which happened around week 10 or 11, then every week became a professional challenge to be our best despite not having a chance at the playoffs.

Every NFL team started the year with two goals—make the playoffs and get to the Super Bowl. Only 10 of 28 teams made the playoffs—and generally you had to win 10 games to earn a spot. Even though effectively eliminated, if not mathematically, we still went out to practice and play with the same intensity as before, partly because we were professionals, but more, I believe, because of the warrior nature of the game. It didn't matter that we weren't going to make the playoffs. When we lined up against the other team on Sunday, adrenaline pumping, crowd roaring, your opponent directly across from you a couple feet—all that mattered was winning and beating that guy across the line. It was immediate and all-consuming. And, we Bengals believed we were building for the next year . . . that we were growing into the kind of team Coach Gregg wanted us to be: disciplined, tough, unyielding.

Our last game of the year was December 21, against the Cleveland Browns. We lost a close game, 27-24. The locker room after the game was pretty quiet. Coach Gregg thanked us for the season, but spoke of unfinished business.

We gathered the next day at Spinney Field to clean out our lockers for the off-season. Most players left town as soon as possible, home for the off-season. Most didn't work in the off-season, having made enough money during the season not to worry about a job. A couple went back to school, trying to get enough credits to graduate (many NFL players were not college graduates, despite spending 5 years in college). Cindy and I, though, had no plans to leave Cincinnati. In fact, in a quiet ceremony with a Presbyterian minister and a witness, with our Ohio marriage license, we were married in the fall of 1980. We told no one, but we had decided to commit to one another and "celebrate" our wedding the following summer, the summer of 1981.

We also moved out of our tiny apartment that fall and bought our first house, at age 22, for $80,000, a standard 4-bedroom, 2½ bath,

2 story at 1616 Eight Mile Road. Our first real home together. We could hardly afford to furnish it on my Bengals pay, so some rooms remained empty for a while. We knew we wanted to have kids, but not yet! Cindy moved us into the house while I was away on a road trip (Kansas City, I think). She hired Big John Movers to move our stuff, and even though their truck broke down in transit, somehow she managed to have us moved in when I got back. This started a long tradition of moves by Cindy and me, and our family, with me managing to be out of town for most of them. How convenient! Though, actually, my participation those rare times that I *was* in town did not prove very helpful.

Our first holiday season in our new home together was, quite frankly, awful. We were in a still-strange city, new house and neighborhood, few friends outside of Bengals teammates, most of whom were gone. I remember driving around a cold and rainy Cincinnati on Christmas Day with Cindy crying in the car, missing her family. Sure we had a Christmas tree and exchanged gifts, but it wasn't the same.

Though most of my teammates were off doing various things in their off-season, I needed structure and a job. I committed to going over to the Bengals practice facility 5 days a week to train with strength coach Kim Wood. There it would usually just be me and Reggie Williams (Dartmouth, linebacker), and Kim put us through some personalized, excruciating workouts. We did some lifting routines that would have us screaming out in pain, cursing at Kim. And, if we'd eaten too close to the workout, running for the bathroom to throw up. I'd worked out hard before but never with this level of intensity. And Reggie was an amazing competitor, an NFL veteran but absolutely committed to getting better. I watched him and learned, and tried to adopt the intensity he brought to every workout.

I also figured out how to get some sort of job each off-season while playing in the NFL. The idea that I could simply use the off-season as a time to train, when that was, at most, 1–2 hours a day, left me bored. Over the course of my time in the NFL, I worked several jobs, including an internship for Cincinnati Milacron (large machine tool company), coach for a junior high track team (where I swore I would never be able to parent 13-year-olds), selling insurance, and working as a paralegal for law firms. The latter job I actually did for several off-seasons, where I was able to work in a law firm and gain valuable experience about what lawyers did and how. Since I was still planning to go to law school after football, it was a great way to experience "the law" before going to school. In Cincinnati, I had the benefit of working for years with attorney, friend and mentor "Coach" Bill Schroeder, who was kind enough to let me do some interesting casework with him.

Cindy too took a job, working in the business office of the local Yellow Pages—RR Donnelly. People tend to think that all professional athletes are wealthy and don't have to work, but in those days of 40 percent marginal tax rates (at our income level), there was not much left of my bonus and salary to live on. And we had bought a house, with a mortgage at a juicy 13.75 percent fixed for 30 years. And we were glad to get that rate because rates were going even higher! So we both worked that first year, and Cindy would do so until she got pregnant and started her MBA. But we are getting ahead of the story.

The big football event of the off-season was my "renegotiation" with the Bengals. Recall I had signed as a free agent for the rookie salary minimum of $25,000, and the next two years at $35,000 and $45,000. But I had surprised everyone and made the team, and even played productively when called on. I mustered up the courage to get an appointment with Mike Brown and make my case. To his credit, he listened and decided to offer me a new 3-year contract at $55,000/$60,000/$70,000. I accepted, realizing I had little bargaining power (he could have said no and held me to the original deal), and I walked out with what I felt was a fair deal, and I vowed I'd work even harder to make an impact on the team. Now that I'd been in The League for a year, and had experienced it, I felt I could play and contribute more. And I set out in the off season to make that happen, working with our strength coach all winter and summer. My goal was to come back to camp in August at a big 260 pounds, in the best shape of my life. And I wanted to compete for more playing time.

The really important event that off-season was our "official" wedding. Cindy and I decided we would put it on and pay for it ourselves, and in the spirit of the early '80s we decided to have the ceremony in a park just north of Cincinnati, overlooking the Ohio River. It was attended by about 50 people, with more coming by our reception at the local Veterans Administration Hall. Cindy made her own wedding dress for under $10. Her friend from college had her mother make us a beautiful wedding cake, which somehow Cindy transported down from Detroit in a small car. Where to store it? The only place with a freezer large enough was a local sports bar, called "The Locker Room," with a walk-in freezer. Somehow appropriate, this bar also served as the site of my very low-key bachelor party the night before our wedding. Understand we had family and friends in from all over, some staying at our house, so it was a bit unusual. And, of course, even after the bachelor party, I got up the day of the wedding and got a good run in—painful though it was. The wedding day itself was a beautiful 75-degree day, and afterward at the reception the guests got a kick out of mingling with the likes of Anthony Munoz, Reggie Williams, and other players. Another unusual twist was the delayed honeymoon, as it was too close to training camp for me to leave town and training for an extended vacation. So, once the guests all left, it was back to the last few weeks of preparation for training camp—this time as an NFL veteran.

As usual, training camp began around the third week of July, when the dog days of the Cincinnati summer were starting to really heat up. But this time, I was more prepared. I had trained with our strength coach all summer, through some gut-busting workouts. I had been "practicing" my grass drills, doing sets of those bastards as part of my workout routine to prepare for the inevitable. And, importantly, I came to training camp a veteran. I had been through a season, knew the coaches, the playbook, the routine, and what it took to be a professional. And this time when I walked onto the Wilmington College campus and into my dorm room for the next 5 weeks, I brought with me the most important piece of equipment I could have (I had learned the hard way last summer): a portable window air conditioner! Oh, it is hard to express the cool bliss this $100 appliance provided to me and my roommate, but at the end of a sweltering day of sweat and stink, to walk into our cool, dimly lit room was like checking into a luxury hotel. Yes, ready for training camp 1981.

Now, veteran or not, I still had to prove myself. Backup offensive linemen are easily replaced by other backup offensive linemen who may be younger, bigger, faster, stronger, or—cheaper. But I had worked hard in the off-season, and I believed no one would exceed my desire, discipline, and commitment. And I also had worked on my trump card, my long snapping, so I was now fully capable of hitting the required times and accuracy demanded in the NFL. Notwithstanding all that: there were another 15 offensive linemen in the meeting room when we started training camp, and again I knew only 8 would get roster spots. I knew for me every practice, play, preseason game, long snap and film session would matter, and that I had to *earn* my spot on the team. Again.

I can't say that training camp in Wilmington was easier this second time around—it was as hard, as physical, as intimidating, as Forrest Gregg, as my first training camp. But it was more familiar. I knew what to expect, I had readied myself for the grass drills, knew the playbook, knew the other players, and knew the drills. I was asked to show up early, with the rookies, as no center was drafted and they needed one in camp for drills. I was OK with the extra work and figured I'd get my "football legs" a bit earlier than the rest of the team by reporting early. No matter how in shape I was or anyone was, the first few days of full-contact drills made us all stiff, sore, and bruised. It was part of life in the NFL.

Perhaps the highlight of the preseason was actually a series of things that happened *outside* of training camp, all related to Rod Horn. Rod had become one of my better friends on the team, despite the fact that he spent most practices beating on my head, as one of two nose tackles on the team. Cindy and I had Rod over for dinner a couple times our rookie year—and she would basically cook for 8 adults and there were no leftovers. One time, after polishing off an entire skillet of Hamburger Helper, with a pound of ground beef, Rod ordered out for pizza. He drove an old gold GMC pickup truck that he refused to upgrade, and seldom filled up the gas tank past half full, resulting in some nervous rides to the airport to make the team plane for away games.

Rod and I were good enough friends that he felt comfortable asking me for a couple of favors as training camp got started in 1981. Well, really the favors were of Cindy, as I would be with Rod in training camp. First, since apparently no Cornhusker in a gold pickup truck can leave home without it, Rod asked if we would "babysit" his shotgun at our house while he was in camp. There was a strict no firearms rule for any NFL camp or facility, and Rod needed a home for his. It was huge and heavy—I remember Cindy could barely lift it, and we looked at each other, wondering where we'd put it. We decided under the bed was as good a place as any. Besides, if she got any more harassing calls (she'd had a couple, and it was not uncommon for players' wives during training camp), then we could picture her in a chair on our porch, shotgun across her knees, daring anyone to bother her.

Favor #2 was a bit more complicated. Rod, country boy that he was, had a pet, of course, and wanted Cindy to look after it until camp was over. The "pet" was a 4-foot bull snake, which Rod kept in a large glass aquarium. Of course he did. Cindy looked at me like I was crazy. But that was the easy part. Mr. Snake had to eat. In came aquarium #2, which contained two mice: Snowflake, the female, and Chainsaw, the stud mouse. Snowflake and Chainsaw each had one job, and they did it well. The resulting progeny were, of course, Mr. Snake's dinner menu. All Cindy had to do was pluck one of them out every few days (careful! Not Snowflake or Chainsaw!) and drop dinner into Mr. Snake's aquarium. Simple, right? Sure, if you were Blake and Rod and headed for training camp. The gun, snake, mice, and Cindy seemed to coexist just fine.

The animals were secluded in an empty bedroom, which stayed shut except when Chef Cindy had to drop in for a feeding. All was great, until I got a call from a very animated wife that on her last dinner visit she realized Mr. Snake was not in his aquarium! *What!* I asked where he was—seemed like a natural question. In between her cursing, I understood Cindy had not engaged in a detailed search, but had run out of the room and shut the door behind her. Great—a live snake loose in the house! And she would have to wait until Rod and I got a one day break from camp to come down and try to find the reptile. One happy wife. But hey, she *did* have a shotgun.

A few days later we did get our break and after a brief search we found Mr. Snake coiled up in a dark, warm closet in the room. Probably hungry. Cindy was quite happy to load up all the wildlife and artillery at the end of training camp and send it along with Rod, where it belonged.

Training camp as always passed slowly, though faster this time than the first. Having been through it once helped me understand the rhythms, the highs and lows, and be prepared for the long haul. I roomed this camp with Billy Glass, a fellow 1980 rookie who had become a friend as we worked our way through our rookie season together as backup linemen. Billy was primarily a guard, me a center, so we shared the same position coach, meetings, line assignments, etc. We both came into camp at Wilmington with the hope to earn more playing time and, ultimately, become starters. You have to remember—every single person on our NFL roster had been a longtime starter and/or star during high school and college. The whole idea of being in a "backup" role was strange, uncomfortable. We all wanted to play!

We fought our way through another brutal Coach Gregg training camp. Interestingly, though, since all the veterans now knew what to expect, we almost took a kind of pride in how hard it was—a shared experience. We looked at rookies and others in a Coach Gregg camp for the first time and wondered if they'd be able to cut it. We all had, we knew we could. That didn't make it easier, though we did know we could do it. I think that attitude, that toughness, permeated the team and brought us all closer. Survive training camp together . . . Nothing could be tougher. We were becoming winners, in the heat and pain of August, as Coach Gregg drove us through endless drills and full-contact practices. We didn't really know it then, but the attitude was being shaped that would lead to a championship season.

The harsh reality of training camp didn't change, of course. That group of 90 was pared to 45 over four weeks. Billy, my friend and training camp roommate, didn't make the final cut. Friendship could be fleeting in the NFL. I wished him well and didn't see him again for over 25 years.

The usual groups of rookies and free agents were cut in large numbers earlier in camp. My practices and time with the starting group had gone well. Toward the end of training camp, my offensive line coach called Blair Bush, last year's starting center, and me, to the side. In a very roundabout way, he was telling us that we were both playing well, but that he was going to work me into the starting lineup more often, more playing time for me. I was excited—all my hard work in the off-season was paying dividends. I'd get to play more in the regular offense, and get much more game time. I attacked the rest of training camp with a sense of purpose and, yes, pride. Not only was I going to make the team again, I'd just been told that I was good enough to start for an NFL team.

We worked through the normal complement of preseason games. We had a new rookie receiver in camp who was turning heads. Tall, skinny, and precocious for a rookie, Chris Collinsworth acted like he belonged on the team from the day he walked in to camp as a second-round draft pick, quickly overshadowing our #1 draft choice with his performance. With Ken Anderson, Archie Griffin, Pete Johnson, Dan Ross, and now a new deep threat at receiver, our offense seemed primed to roll. Our defense was hard-nosed and stingy. We broke camp with a sense of optimism and toughness that had been honed over the weeks of hell in Wilmington. Then, as we were practicing on the Astroturf of Riverfront Stadium in Cincinnati, just when things were going so well for me, the unexpected happened. We were running a pass-blocking drill, where the five offensive linemen would work against four defensive linemen. The defense ran their line stunts and crosses, and we would practice picking up the stunts and protecting our quarterback. In these drills, then, basically nine large men, 250 pounds or more, are moving quickly and with power in a very small area. The offensive linemen brace and jam and pass off the defensive linemen to each other, creating a pocket for the quarterback. It takes skill, timing, strength, and some anticipation of what the defensive linemen *will* do. And remember, the defensive line is moving *forward*, while we offensive linemen are backing up, holding the line, "giving ground with dignity."

I was in my center spot, working through the blocking progression, jamming one defensive tackle and braced against him, preparing to pass him off to my guard. As I was braced, right leg set to hold off the charging 275 pounder in front of me, another 275 pounder came flying in from my right, being pushed to the ground at full speed. But instead of the ground, he first fell into the side of my right knee. I felt a pop, a flash of pain, yelled, and went down, holding my knee. Could have happened to any lineman in any practice on any day, but today it happened to me. I had been extraordinarily lucky from an injury standpoint throughout my football career. Very lucky. Had my luck run out? In the few seconds I was on the ground these things ran through my head, including that if I was injured, I might not make the team. Injured reserve was a sure way for backup offensive linemen to eventually be released. I tried to jump back up, and "walk it off."

The trainer was there, examining me. It didn't seem too bad, but it hurt, and I couldn't keep practicing. I feared the worst and went in to be examined by the trainer and later the doctor (no MRIs in these days). The exam was physical manipulation of the knee to see if I had damaged it somehow. Diagnosis—sprained medial collateral ligament. The good news was no tear, no surgery. The bad news was I'd be out of practice for a couple of weeks or more, and then work back in over the next couple of weeks to full strength, assuming I didn't injure it further. I was bitterly disappointed. I had been on the verge of getting more playing time when the season started after the final preseason game. Now, not only would I miss the last preseason game, and the opener, but it would be unlikely that I'd be able to earn my way back into the starting rotation once the season started and the lineups were set. This proved true.

I missed a couple weeks of practice before I could tape up and brace my knee enough to get out and start practicing again, but really four weeks to 100 percent. By that time, we'd won our first two games (which I had to watch from the sideline—in full gear but for emergency duty only), and with the starting unit playing well together, there was no need to shuffle the mix, so I resumed my backup role.

But what a difference a year makes. Our confidence as a team was high. We'd been in the Coach Gregg system for two training camps, and had the confidence, and more importantly the desire, to beat anyone we played. We had beaten the Pittsburgh Steelers twice the year before, and we as a team really did believe we would take it to the next level this year. We started out 5-2, losing two close ones, but winning one in overtime and flashing just how good we might be. For our eighth game, we traveled to New Orleans, and lost to a bad team. That loss was a turning point. Coach Gregg had warned all of us about New Orleans, night life, curfew, etc. Most listened to him. A few didn't, missed curfew, and made Coach Gregg furious. With good reason. He used it as a way to question what we wanted as individuals and as a team. Were we ready and willing to make the sacrifices needed to be a winner, to be excellent, week in and week out? Would we put the team first? Or would a few of us let the rest down, would a few weaken the whole team effort? We were embarrassed as professionals. I do think we used that to pull together, and we reeled off 5 straight wins, in dominant fashion, and suddenly we were 10-3 and in control of the AFC Central Division, and one of the best teams in the NFL.

Our fans were going crazy. Recall that this was the first year of our new striped uniforms. They had been met with some skepticism and heckling, but now: Stripe me, baby! Striped faces, striped shirts, striped cars, striped bodies, even striped beer. Yes, our local brewery, Hudepohl, had come out with a beer to celebrate the team's success. The fans had taken up a raucous cheer in the middle of this season, which soon filled the stadium: "Who dey?! Who dey?! Who dey think gonna beat dem Bengals?!" Over and over, louder and louder. Hudepohl created an orange/black tiger-striped beer can, called it "Hu-Dey Beer," and promptly sold out (it was not very good beer—but who cared?!).

As players, we loved the winning. After that first interminable year of 10 losses, here we were on the other side of winning and it felt great. Our fans wanted to see us. We were recognized around town, not to scorn but to admire. Everyone loves a winner—that statement is so true, especially in American sports. We went on a tear through November, seemingly unstoppable. We were leading our division comfortably, but were in a very close race with other top teams for the top playoff spot in the AFC and home field advantage. We started talking about the playoffs quietly—out loud we kept saying one game at a time, but that is hard to actually do when things are going so well.

Our wake-up call came in our first game in December, against San Francisco, at home. We were flat and got our butts kicked. You can only imagine how Coach Gregg used *that* performance as a motivator! Especially with the Steelers coming up the following week, in Pittsburgh. I am sure he used one of his many "speeches" during the week after the loss, leading up to the Steelers game. After playing with Coach Gregg for 6 years, I and others realized he had a repertoire of motivational speeches that he could use whenever the occasion demanded during the season. For example, if we were up big at halftime and feeling confident, he would talk at halftime about playing the second half as intensely as the first, never to let up on the opponent. This would usually end with the story about capturing an opossum in a sack, and then, to be sure the critter wasn't going to get away, you "put a foot on its neck and yanked on its tail." "Got it?!! Now get out there and finish off these guys" (the other team). We'd take the field after halftime totally fired up, yelling "Yank on the tail! Yank on the tail!" The other team had to think we were crazy.

But this week Coach Gregg probably would have resorted to one of his standards, a rant I think I heard at least once every year I played for him, and one of my favorites. It was all about producing results, or failing to do so. He would usually use a recent performance as the catalyst for the speech, a bad recent performance where, in his view, players had not been performing well, doing what it took to win—in short, not producing results. With eyes flashing intensity, Coach Gregg would slam off the projector in the middle of a film session. He'd turn around to the team and stand fully to his 6 four 4, 250-pound height: "I don't know what you guys are doing out there. No intensity, no desire to win. Do you think you can just go through the motions and get what you want? I got news for you—you won't. In this business, in the NFL, you are paid to produce—on the field. And it's the same in real life too. Maybe some of you guys think you can marry a rich woman and take it easy. But let me tell you all somethin': even if you do [marry a rich woman], you *still gotta produce.*" Oh, that was sweet! I'll remember it always, and have recited it on numerous occasions. His simple message—there is no easy way to win—winners have to produce. And don't ever forget it. I never did.

We went into Pittsburgh on a mission, to prove we Bengals were the real deal. The playoff road still went through those Steelers, even if they weren't as dominant as before. It was up to us to show we belonged in the elite group of NFL teams, and to do it we needed to win on the road, against the Steelers. The stadium, as always, was filled to capacity with black and gold fanatics. Their offense wasn't very good, but they still had a ferocious defense that was whipped into a frenzy by the crowd. And it was still led by one of the best middle linebackers in the game, Jack Lambert.

Lambert was tallish for a middle linebacker, strong, mean, fast. And all at once. He'd line up over the center, 2–3 yards off the ball, and glare at the opposing QB . . . or anyone else who dared look him in the face. He'd snarl, with his grin missing a couple of front teeth.

Then he'd move along the line looking for the ball and deliver a punishing blow. He was the leader of a tough defense.

The game was a heavyweight fight, Pittsburgh not wanting to concede anything to us upstart Bengals, and us upstart Bengals trying to break through the Steel curtain. At one point in a close game, one of those plays happened, a play that tips one team one way and the other team the other way. Our QB Ken Anderson flipped a little screen pass out to our truck of a fullback, Pete Johnson. Pete was about 6 feet tall and weighed in the range of 250 pounds and up. When he got going forward, he was fast and like a large bowling ball. He took in the pass from Anderson and headed up the field. Lambert moved out to stop him, and for a moment we all saw—the whole stadium saw—that there was going to be a collision—a brutal collision—and only one winner.

Johnson veered directly at the onrushing Lambert, not making any move to miss him. He hit Lambert full in the chest with his helmet, and Lambert pinged off him and to the ground as though hit by a truck. Johnson kept running until eventually dragged down from behind. The stadium was quiet, except the Bengal sideline. We were going nuts, realizing we were going to beat the Steelers and go on to the playoffs. Who Dey?! indeed!

Our final game of the regular season was away, against the Atlanta Falcons. A win would seal the best record in the AFC for us, and home field advantage for the playoffs. An important game, but one I remember for a very different reason. The culture of football is many things, including competition, power, pain, denial (of injury), machismo, extreme highs and lows, fear (of losing, of being cut), and many more. One of them involves a culture of young, strong men in their prime, with money. And, yes, that often can attract a variety of women to those young men, or at least the opportunity should the players want it. Now I always did my best to stay out of situations where this could even remotely be a problem, mainly because I was happily married but also because I just didn't want any part of that side of football. And so whenever we were on the road, staying in our team hotel, I normally arrived with the team, attended practices and meetings, and otherwise stayed holed up in my room and out of trouble.   My roommate was a young backup QB who was single and quite enjoying that fact. We were in this respect somewhat opposites, and I suspect that Coach Gregg put us together for that very reason—me as the settling influence on my roommate. My normal Saturday evening routine before a Sunday away game was: team or position meetings, team dinner, then retire to my room to watch two TV shows that were on *every* Saturday night: *Love Boat* and *Fantasy Island*. Like clockwork, Cindy could (and would) call my room to catch up, usually with the *Love Boat* on in the background. My "roomie" was horrified and either stayed out until curfew (11 p.m.) or tried to sleep through it. Remember, these were the days of minimal cable, with three network stations, so options were very limited. This was our routine, and even though Cindy was OK with it, I'm sure it was hard for her to see me off on road games where I'd stay at hotels where there were inevitably opportunistic women looking for lonely players. She had nothing to worry about, though in Atlanta that weekend she had a moment of doubt.

At the normal time, Cindy called to the hotel in Atlanta and asked to speak to Blake Moore. The hotel operator put her through, and on the other end was a woman with a sweet Southern accent. "Hello?" Cindy, taken aback, said "who is this?!" The lady, equally shocked, apparently responded similarly. Cindy said she wanted to speak to her husband, Blake Moore. The lady responded that *she* was Blake Moore's wife, and *who* was Cindy and *why* was she calling for her husband? And she hung up.

Now, I can only imagine what flashed through Cindy's mind at the moment. Remember, there we were, in a hotel in Atlanta only two hours from my hometown of Chattanooga. She told me her mind was a bit numb when the Southern sweetie hung up on her. To Cindy's credit, she redialed and asked the hotel operator what was going on, why she had been connected to the wrong room, and "How many Blake Moores are registered in your [damn] hotel, anyway?" The operator checked, and, yes, indeed, did find that *two* Blake Moores were registered at the hotel, and that Cindy had been connected to the wrong room. Of course, all this was happening while I was lying in my hotel room, watching another scintillating episode of *Love Boat* (would Gopher ever have a date? Would Doc commit love malpractice? Would Captain Stubing run the boat aground? Alas, no . . .).

When the phone rang for our regular call, I had a rather animated wife on the line, who told the above story and was awfully glad I had picked up the phone on her *second* try for Blake *without* a female guest. With the sounds of *Love Boat* in the background, a potentially distrusting moment became a good story that we would share many times about our young marriage and NFL road trips.

Oh, yeah, and we beat Atlanta and finished up a great regular season, 12-4. What a difference a year makes! We had all bought into the tough, disciplined approach of Coach Gregg and had pulled together as a team with one goal: win—playoffs—Super Bowl.

My role over the year, after recovering from my early season injury, was backup to Bush, our starting center, and the offensive line positions. I also played on certain special teams and would sub in for injuries or mop-up duty at the ends of games. Not the life of a starter, but in the mix, and always ready to go when and if called. And just like that, in my second year in the NFL we were headed to the playoffs with the home field advantage, needing two wins to get in the Super Bowl. This was big—not just being in the playoffs, but also financially. This year my full season pay was $55,000 (after my renegotiation in the off-season). By earning a spot in the playoffs, each player also received an additional bonus depending on how far we advanced.

Because of our record, we had a first round bye. If we won the first divisional playoff game, we'd each get $9,000 ($5,000 if we lost). Winning the next game, the AFC Championship, was worth $18,000 ($9,000 for losers). And winning the Super Bowl was worth another $36,000 ($18,000 for losers). As you do the math, you can see that the playoff money, potentially, was worth almost as much as my full season of pay. Nice incentive to have, for sure. But despite the money, really at this level it is the winning—the chance to be world champions—that drove us. Once you walked onto the field in a playoff game, knowing a win advances us, a loss and we're done—every player was intent on doing everything he had to do to win.

The intensity level ratcheted up to levels I'd never experienced. All pre-game routines became amplified. We wouldn't take the field until Jim LeClair had gotten loud and given a little speech, or until Dan Ross could be heard barfing in the bathroom. We committed to ourselves and one another that we'd do whatever it took to win—*whatever* it took.

Our first playoff opponent was the Buffalo Bills, who won their wild card game and a ticket to play us at home. They were good, but not as good as we were, especially at home. Still, it was the first time most of us Bengals had ever been in a playoff game, and so we were good enough to win, though not great. Final score, 28-21, but not as close as that sounds. As the game wound down to its conclusion we all began to realize that the next week we'd be playing in the AFC Championship game, right here in Cincinnati, for the chance to go to the Super Bowl.

Up until this point in the year we had carefully avoided talking about the Super Bowl—we talked of winning one game at a time, making the playoffs, then winning a playoff game. Now, it was right in front of us, unavoidable in all aspects of our lives—work, TV news, press coverage, neighbors. Our opponent coming to town was the San Diego Chargers, who had one of the most amazing offenses the NFL had ever seen. They threw the ball all over the field, scoring prolifically. We'd played them earlier in the year in San Diego and had beaten them in an offensive shoot-out, where some 60 points were scored and almost 1,000 yards of total offense run up. What defense?

But this time San Diego was coming to Cincinnati . . . in January. And so was another potent factor: a cold front. But this was no ordinary cold front. The predictions that January week in Cincinnati were for frigid temperatures and winds that would threaten and break records.

As we went through our practice week—outside in the cold, of course—it continued to get colder and colder. We were practicing in 20 and 30 below wind chill weather, pulling on all the cold-weather gear we could. And in those low-tech days of clothing, that usually meant multiple layers of tee shirts and long underwear until you could hardly move around. We began wearing scuba-type gloves, thick neoprene which was fine for most linemen but was troublesome to say the least for players who had to handle the ball—including us centers. Of course, Coach Gregg loved it, loved the fact that it was going to be a frozen field and icy-cold weekend for the warm weather San Diego Chargers. And so we practiced a regular week in those conditions, with little allowance made for the cold.

Two days before the game, at our Friday practice, we practiced in the stadium by the icy cold Ohio River. The wind was whistling through the stadium and swirling around, creating wind chills of minus 40 degrees or worse. It was difficult to function or think, so consumed we were with merely surviving the cold.

We gathered as we always did at a Marriott outside the city the Saturday night before the game. The weather predictions were dire— perhaps one of the coldest days in the history of Cincinnati, and windy. There were scattered rumors of the game being rescheduled, but we largely ignored those because (i) the NFL played in all weather (except lightning) and (ii) the TV and travel and other schedules were set. Many of us drove to the hotel, so we were warned to allow plenty of time to drive into the stadium in case we had trouble starting our cars. Many of us had relatives in town for the big game and wondered if they should go or watch on TV. People were being warned of the danger of prolonged exposure.

Game day broke bright, sunny . . . and colder than even predicted. The absolute air temperature at game time was minus 9, but with 25+ mph winds, the recorded wind chill at the time was 59 below, making this the coldest game in NFL history (still), and even colder than the famed "Ice Bowl" in Green Bay (which Coach Gregg had played in).

Somehow, I got my Chevrolet Citation to turn over and start, and drove down to the stadium from the hotel, worrying all the way there that the car might simply grind to a halt from the cold. The streets were almost empty, the weather keeping everyone inside.

We went through our normal pre-game routines, or tried to, getting taped and dressed as usual. Only this time, we were doing extra things, like coating any exposed skin with Vaseline (to prevent frostbite), and wrapping our toes in saran wrap to help hold the warmth in. Many of us even pulled on the queen-size panty hose that had been provided to help keep our legs warm under our game pants—yes, I have no shame in admitting I put those on and any other warm gear I could find. Ear holes in helmets were taped up to keep the wind out. Guys figured out how to wear some kind of cloth or skull cap underneath the helmet for a little added warmth. At some point, in an act of bravery, foolishness, or utter insanity, our five starting offensive linemen decided they would take the field and play bare-armed, short sleeves, for the pure intimidation factor. We backup linemen—we layered on everything we could!

And when it came time to go out for "warm-ups," (that's funny) nothing we had done or put on prepared us for the steel wall of Arctic air that seemed to circle around in the wind from every direction. Within seconds, eyes teared up, skin began to tingle, toes started to go numb. Having practiced in similar conditions all week, we knew we'd survive, and we tried to run through a normal warm-up. Toughest part was taking off the gloves to work on long-snapping drills—then I could *really* feel the cold in my exposed fingers, numb in seconds.

We saw the Chargers take the field for their warm-ups. I noticed the huge end zone doors in the stadium were open to the Ohio River, where the wind howled into the tunnel created there and shot out onto the field at the Chargers. They "warmed-up" for 5 or 10 minutes (30 was normal) and retreated to their locker room. The gamesmanship had begun, and we stayed out for our entire warm-up period, as usual.

We came out for the opening kickoff full of excitement, tempered by the playing conditions. The stadium, despite the cold and warnings to fans, was almost full. My mom, Cindy, and brothers were there for the game. Some idiotic fans were stripped to the waist, upper torsos painted in black and orange stripes. Some had to be treated for hypothermia. The men's urinals *inside* the stadium froze up. We had rudimentary "heated benches" on the sidelines, which were basically hollow fiberglass benches with propane heaters blasting hot air into the space under the bench. Didn't work. Players on the sidelines, in an effort to warm up their feet (me included), held their shoes/feet directly in the propane heat blast, which only served to start to melt the rubber soles rather than warming up the toes.

My role in the game was special teams, meaning I would have to run in for a kickoff return here or a point after there or a field goal try. After freezing on the sideline, it was hard to go in for one play, and then hope you didn't get hit too hard because the pain in the cold was unbearable.

Our starting offensive line, bare arms and steaming breath, controlled the Chargers. Ken Anderson managed the offense and got us 27 points. The high-powered Charger offense was, literally, frozen. The ball was like a cold stone, hard for their QB Dan Fouts to throw with his usual distance and accuracy. By the time we moved into the fourth quarter, we knew the result was inevitable. We were going to win, and we were going to the Super Bowl. Who Dey?!

It took us days to warm back up, but the excitement that we'd won and were going to the Super Bowl helped us forget the pain. We had two weeks to prepare for our meeting with the San Francisco 49ers, their first Super Bowl as well. We had lost to them in the regular season, but we Bengals were in as the "favorites" in the days leading up to the game. The big game was scheduled to be played in the Pontiac Silverdome, just outside Detroit. The first time the NFL had scheduled the Super Bowl in a northern city, given the weather concerns. No matter—the game would be in a dome—how bad could it be? Well, Super Bowl XVI would show them.

In January 1982, the Super Bowl was a big deal, but not really the megaspectacle it is today. We were going to Super Bowl XVI, number 16, so only 15 short years ago the first one was played as almost an experiment, to see how the U.S. TV audience would respond. Well, that had worked out pretty well, the Super Bowl now regularly commanding the largest or one of the largest U.S. (and world) TV audiences, not just for a sporting event, but for *any* event. Recall also that cable TV was still in its infancy, so really there were three dominant networks (ABC/NBC/CBS), only one of which got to carry "the game."

After we won the AFC Championship game, and after thawing out, we met as a team to review our Super Bowl schedule. The game itself was two weeks from our Sunday win over the Chargers. The Bengals brass, never having been to a Super Bowl before, consulted with other teams (rumor was the Steelers) to see how they had run their schedule and logistics. For you see, this game required the entire team, equipment and all, to be in Detroit for most of the week leading up to the game. The media frenzy and hoopla required feeding, and we were the grist for the sports mill that week, so that meant we'd be spending most of the week in a hotel outside Detroit, near the Pontiac Silverdome.

Coach Gregg wanted us to be on a practice schedule as close to "normal" as possible for the week leading up to the game, so that meant he wanted us there and ready to go Wednesday morning. Factoring in travel and various required media events (more on that later), we flew up on our chartered plane to Detroit the Sunday or Monday before the game. Players only—no wives or family. Coach Gregg wanted no distractions (ha!)—this was a business trip, with only one acceptable outcome—a win. And we shared his view— yes, we were excited to be playing in the Super Bowl, but most of the team traveled to Detroit with one thing in mind—win the damn game. Fight through all the distractions, try to run a normal practice schedule, prepare, and then execute on game day.

To that end, once we arrived in Detroit, we had a very controlled schedule, from morning meetings, meals, practice, more meetings. We had little downtime, and besides, we were in a suburb of Detroit, in January, in the middle of a horrible U.S. automobile recession/depression—not a lot to do anyway. In an effort to keep our routine as normalized as possible, our strength coach even had our entire weight room of Nautilus equipment and weights trucked to Pontiac and set up for us to use during the week.

But no matter what we did, this was no ordinary week. On one of our first days there, we participated in the designated "media day," a day when we players went out on the Silverdome field and milled around for an hour or two, while the dozens and dozens of press and media folks from all over the country had their chance to interview any Bengal player or coach, and ask the same questions over and over again of the star players (Griffin, Anderson, Collinsworth, Johnson, Munoz), and occasionally interview someone else. The scene was madness. Like a mob of ants on honey, the stars would be surrounded by microphones, notebooks, and shouted questions, trying to patiently answer all the requests. Coaches too. Now me, Blake Moore, backup center and lineman from the College of Wooster, went largely unnoticed. No mobs gathered around me, so I had the chance to sit back, largely unmolested, and observe. There was Ken Anderson surrounded by 30 reporters, Coach Gregg with 20, Chris Collinsworth, the star rookie (and great interview), with 50. I wandered around, listening in, making myself available. Finally I plopped down on an empty bench on the field and just sat and watched.

Surprisingly, a camera crew and reporter approached me—why? Ah—they wanted to get the perspective of a player who was *not* surrounded by reporters, *not* a star. Well, they came to the right place for that. I shared some personal background and some observations with the reporter, on film. Very brief. They went their way, and after awhile the session was over. Later in the week, I was told my interview was actually broadcast on *Night Line*, a nationally broadcast late-night news show, in a segment on Super Bowl mania. My first national TV interview!

Every day, back at our hotel, we also had designated media time. This meant the entire team was scheduled to appear in one of the hotel conference rooms, where we would all sit at a table with our names on the table so the reporters could decide who they wanted to interview. For me, this meant usually sitting and chatting with my other teammates who weren't among the desired few. We weren't bitter about it; it's just the way it was. In fact, for the players who had to work through a dozen reporters every day, it had to be tough.

And in the middle of all this, Coach Gregg was doing his best to keep us together and focused as a team. Never mind this was Super Bowl week—we got taped up, full gear, and went out on Wednesday for a regular full-contact practice. We lifted weights like it was the middle of the season. We had meetings, and more film sessions. The game plan was rehearsed backward and forward. We had played these 49ers before, and even though we lost, we were extremely confident we were the better team, and that we would show that on Sunday.

The intensity of the week started to build, magnified by all the attention with which we were bombarded every waking hour. Each day we'd take our team rental cars over to the Silverdome for our designated practice time (coordinated so we wouldn't be there with the 49ers). We'd run through a normal Wednesday, Thursday, and Friday practice. Except nothing was "normal." We had lively practices, with contact, telling ourselves we were outworking the 49ers, who were rumored to be taking a much-looser approach to their preparation. In fact, the story was that their head coach Bill Walsh met his team at the hotel in some sort of disguise, and that at some point he rode up on a big motorcycle. Couldn't really see Coach Gregg doing that—not his personality, nor the personality of our team—largely a collection of talented players, but not superstars. We derived our success through hard work, discipline, and team play.

The week passed quickly, and we were all ready for the game to begin, anyway. Coach Gregg relented and allowed wives to join us the Saturday night before the game. Not sure of the reasoning, there—I know I was hyper, couldn't sleep, and was a pain to be around. I'm sure others were the same. And I wasn't even starting the game, but I wanted to be ready for all contingencies, knowing all the assignments for the offensive line, every position. Even though the game was to be played in a dome, weather was a factor. We all had family and friends coming to the game, and the forecast for Detroit in January was—surprise!—cold, with a winter storm predicted for Saturday night and into Super Bowl Sunday. Thus, we all were also dealing with family and friends traveling, arriving, wanting to see "their Bengals," Super Bowl tickets, etc.

As players, we each got 10 tickets to the game, with the possibility to buy more if available (they generally were not available). Tickets were $50, but, of course, were scalpable for much more—maybe $200–$300 in those days (a far cry from the market prices of today, though remember this was still young in Super Bowl years, and the NFL marketing machine was not what it is today).

After a fitful night, Super Bowl Sunday finally dawned, as bleak and as dreary as a Detroit winter morning can be. In fact, the winter storm turned out to be an ice storm. Flights were cancelled, people couldn't make it to the game, roads were an icy mess. Oh, yeah, the NFL must have been saying to itself—*this* is why we usually have these damn things in California or Florida or New Orleans. *Duh*.

We climbed on our team buses for the drive to the stadium after a last set of meetings and pre-game meal. The morning seemed to drag on forever, and it was a relief to finally be on the way to the game. Not a lot was said on the bus. The nature of the game, the scale, the stakes, were all sinking in. Players were buried in their own thoughts and last-minute mental preparations. Our bus was delayed, even with police escort, due to the bad weather. But they couldn't start the game without us.

Finally arriving, we went through our pre-game routines as best we could. Taping ankles, stretching, last-minute coaching reviews, Danny Ross puking in the back bathroom—we were ready. Going out on the field for pre-game warm-ups was surreal. The stadium was still filling up, but we also knew that the TV audience would be enormous, maybe a record. Each team worked through their drills. The fans (over 81,000) slowly filled the stadium after their fight through the ice. The atmosphere was electric, adrenaline-filled. It made all our other games seem like practice games. We were as ready as we could be, just dying to get out on the field and actually *play* the game.

And then, it seemed, in a flash, it was over. I played on special teams, most notably the kickoff return wedge. We wedge guys (my fellow offensive lineman Mike Obravic and I were the two-man wedge) had *explicit*, nonnegotiable instructions *never* to touch the football. If it came to us or at us we were to get away from it and let one of the "skill" players handle the ball.

Now, the 49ers for this game employed a kickoff strategy we hadn't seen before: the squib kick, where their kicker kicked the ball in a low-line drive, skipping and hopping crazily down the turf right at us—the wedge. And each time, Mike and I would dutifully do as instructed, avoid the rolling ball, and allow our return man to, well, what he did was usually bobble, fumble, or otherwise mishandle the ball resulting in bad field position after no return. I could have *fallen* on the damn ball as it squibbed past me and we'd have been better off—but no—we were coached to do what we were coached to do, and so sacrificed field position, rather than adjust to the new situation (a leadership lesson here for sure!).

Before we knew it, it was halftime, and after various miscues, turnovers by us, and good plays by the 49ers and some guy named Joe Montana—we were down 20-0. 20-0! The 49ers ran off the field at halftime through the same tunnel as we did, and some of them were laughing *at* us and running tilted to one side or another, mimicking what the weight of their soon-to-be-won Super Bowl rings would feel like on their hands. Well, that was noticed and used as motivation by us at halftime, but I must say, we were in a bit of shock too. Halfway through the biggest game of our lives, and we were getting beaten . . . badly.

We rallied, we scored. We got the game to 20-7. Then, with the ball on their 3 yard line first and goal to go, in the 3rd quarter, we failed to score. Fullback up the middle, twice, and stopped. Swing past to our running back, who was stopped. Then, 4th and one, and fullback into the line—no gain, no score. It was the turning point. We scored again early in the 4th quarter, but two more field goals by the 49ers put the game out of reach despite a late score by us for the final of 26-21. *Final?! We lost?* We couldn't believe it. I was in shock, we all were, as the 49ers yelled and celebrated all around us on the field.

We wandered around a bit, then filed into a very quiet locker room. Coach Gregg, visibly angry and frustrated, did his best to control his emotions and congratulate us on a fine season, the finest by any Bengals team ever. But we all knew, and would always know, just as I know as I write these words—*we could have won the Super Bowl*—and we didn't. We all were required to attend the after-party at the hotel for the team, families, coaches. It was tough to do, not much to party about. We tried to console each other with "we'll be backs" or "if onlys" or "we were the better team," but really, we lost. And that pain has never entirely gone away. A lesson I would never forget.

The evening finally ended. We filtered back to our rooms, sad and deflated. Sleep was not easy. I felt, and assume others felt, that we'd just come up one quarter short. The next morning broke cold and wet and rainy. We all (players, coaches, family members) climbed on the team buses for the ride to the airport. There, our flight was delayed, so we sat on the bus with little to do but wait. Coach Gregg was on our bus. The mood was as dreary as the weather. There was no laughter, no chitchat. Small children started to get restless, then upset, then cried at the delay and discomfort. After about an hour of this, Cindy and I looked at each other and decided we wouldn't be having children for *a while!* (Note for the record: we were pregnant a few months later.)

When we finally arrived in Cincinnati, it was as if the weather, clouds, and cold rain had followed us from Detroit. We filed off the plane and onto team buses again, for now we had a scheduled appearance around noon in Cincinnati city square, a celebration of our Super Bowl appearance. It was supposed to be a victory celebration, but you go with what you've got, so now it was an "appearance". None of us were in the mood. The bus trip was long and slow. At least one player's child had to use the bathroom, but these being city buses there were no facilities, so he did what he had to do—peed on the bus floor.

We arrived at the square, and as we got off the bus and moved up to the podium, the noise of the crowd swelled. For there *was* a crowd, a *big* crowd, and they cheered us with pride and joy. It was just the tonic we needed after the last 24 hours, basking in our fans' appreciation for a good year. And two or three of us spoke to the crowd. I, for some reason, was asked to speak, and with no prepared remarks simply thanked Cincinnati for being such a great city to play in, and then I looked out at the crowd and said something like "We got a taste of the Super Bowl, but not what we wanted, and we plan to come back next year and win it." Sounded good—little did I know how hard it would be to do.

And so began my second off-season as a player. I had taken Paul Brown's words to heart from my rookie training camp, and I always had some sort of job lined up in the off-season. Making around $50,000 a year playing ball, about half that after taxes, was comfortable but not "rich." Over the course of my off-seasons in Cincinnati, I worked: for Cincinnati Milacron (a machine tool manufacturer) as a management trainee; paralegal for a Cincinnati law firm through my own little legal services company I set up; life insurance salesman (not for long—I wasn't very good at it!); junior high school track coach.

Now this last job, which paid $400 for the entire season (8 weeks), I took so I could see if coaching was something I might want to do in the future. It was a small suburban junior high school outside of Cincinnati. I coached both girls and boys, seventh-and eighth-graders. One of the first things I noticed as I took the job—the school had *no track*, and in fact the only place for the team to run was around the roughly paved traffic circle in front of the school. This posed some problems from a training standpoint. My shot putters practiced throwing from a parking spot into the grassy lawn. We had a couple of old hurdles to use, and some beat-up batons. But largely, I discovered, this was an exercise in after-school care, and I only had a *few* kids there who were somewhat serious about the track part. This became very clear to me when we all climbed on the school bus together to go to our first track meet, and I spent most of the trip defusing seventh- and eighth-grade hormonal incidents, arguments, and bickering. But still, I organized the "team" as best I could, teaching the basics that I knew (I had done track in high school and college, just not at a high level.)

Highlight of the season? We were heading to a track meet down busy Interstate 75, when our bus conked out and had to pull over at the side of the road (what is it with me and busses?). While I sent the driver to organize a rescue, I had the whole team out by the side of the Interstate, in the grass, warming up so we'd be ready to go when we got to the meet. What discipline! Didn't lose a single athlete that day, to injury or traffic.

The other thing brewing after our Super Bowl was labor unrest. Our collective bargaining agreement with the NFL was up, and there was talk of strikes and lockouts. I wasn't sure what to make of all that, and really thought it would be resolved and we'd play the games as usual. None of the players really made enough money to have a "strike fund," so we all just went about our business in the off-season. Part of that business for the Bengal players was obviously making babies, because several of us got pregnant during the off-season.

More players stayed in town after our winning year, and one of our off-season activities, unofficially, was to go on the road and play charity basketball games around Ohio and southern Indiana. I loved doing this partly because I liked to play basketball, and partly for the camaraderie with the other Bengals who would play. We played in little gyms, high school and otherwise, all over the state. We even made some trips up to play against the Cleveland Browns players, which was entertaining for players and fans alike—and those could get a bit competitive.

Once we played in a donkey basketball game, which, to my surprise, did include real donkeys on a basketball court. We straddled the stubborn beasts, some of us so tall our feet would drag on the floor. We drew a crowd for that one, and it was quite the sight to see these premier athletes astride gray/brown donkeys who completely ignored anything the rider asked them to do. Life in the NFL.

And in another of these charity games, over in southern Indiana, we played against a team that, at that time, had the tallest player who'd ever played in college—at 7 foot 7. I think he weighed 175 pounds—we were afraid we might break him, us 6 foot 5, 270 pounders. But one thing we learned playing basketball in the Hoosier state—charity games or not—they come to play! We had to get our game faces on when we crossed the border into Indiana, and we had some pretty intense "charity" games there.

Cindy and I got pregnant around May that 1982 off-season. Not sure what changed our minds after the Super Bowl bus discussion, but there you go. We were excited for this new chapter in our lives, though I must say, at age 24, I'm not sure we really knew what we were doing! Well, I didn't.

Cindy had been working for a local company, and now decided to start graduate school, her MBA, at Xavier University. Not only would Cindy be one of the very few women getting her MBA, she was *certainly* the only pregnant woman in her MBA classes at Xavier University.

The off-season flew by. Charity basketball games, the excitement of being prospective parents, working as a paralegal, and training . . . always training and lifting. I put on more weight and strength in the summer and felt I was coming into camp in great shape and ready to contend again for a starting spot. As this was now my third training camp, I was comfortable in the routines and expectations. It was still the same hellish four weeks of training camp—*that* never changed. But I knew what to do and how to prepare, and was ready for my third NFL season.

Training camp was relatively uneventful—we worked hard and I felt ready to push for a starting spot, but I sensed coming off a Super Bowl there was little appetite for shaking up the roster, so I accepted my role as backup with "team first" enthusiasm.

There was, however, a very scary event that happened while I was away in Wilmington. Cindy by this time was about three months pregnant with Lauren, our first. And her pregnancy was anything but easy. We joke that she felt lousy basically from conception to birth, but that is not much of an exaggeration. Her morning sickness was so severe that at times the doctor was concerned she was not getting enough to eat (and keeping it down). I got a call during training camp that she had gotten so sick and dehydrated that she had to go into the hospital for a few days. I was relieved from camp for a quick visit to make sure everything was OK, but she got some anti-nausea medication and sent me back to camp. Still, imagine going through that alone, with your husband ensconced in training camp and no other family nearby. We were both glad when camp was over, I was back home, and she was at least able to start eating enough (for two).

The labor dispute rhetoric continued to fly around the locker room and the press. Ed Garvey, our union chief at the time, made the rounds to every team, garnering support for a strike, if needed. We dutifully attended and voted yes to strike if we couldn't reach a deal, none of us really knowing what that might mean.

The regular season opened on a blazingly hot day in September in Cincinnati, our first game after the Super Bowl. The stadium was packed, and we were hosting division rivals the Houston Oilers. As it turned out, I was the starter for this game at center—some minor injury to Bush, I think. The nose guard for Houston was an enormous guy. He had arms and legs like tree trunks. Not real fast or quick, but he could bull-rush you back into the quarterback in a hurry if he got leverage on you. We fought each other all day long in the heat and humidity—I was exhausted but victorious—individually I played well, and we won the game. I really did feel at this point that

I "belonged" in the NFL, as much as a free agent from Wooster ever really could.

The next weekend we were in Pittsburgh for the Steelers, and I was back in my usual special teams/backup role. We lost a tough game to them in overtime, and then, one or two days later, it happened. The NFL Players Association, our union, called a strike, and the owners/ NFL responded with a lockout, meaning effectively that there was all of a sudden no more football. Players had no access to team facilities or training or coaches. We were simply and suddenly unemployed. No game checks. No union funds. No games. No football.

In the beginning, we hoped it would settle quickly, but as the days and weeks wore on, the hope for a quick settlement faded. The sides were far apart, with the players demanding something novel called "revenue sharing," and the owners saying "never." [The NFL currently has a revenue sharing agreement that is a model for pro sports.]

In the first couple weeks our QB Ken Anderson and a few others organized team workouts over at the University of Cincinnati stadium. In the beginning they were well attended, with good spirit: we wanted to keep our Super Bowl form and get back to the playoffs. Some of the assistant coaches even made some unofficial appearances, just to "observe" (they weren't supposed to have any player contact). But after a couple weeks, and little optimism that the strike would resolve soon, attendance petered out and eventually players went about their business as best they could. The word went around that we players were actually entitled to apply for unemployment insurance, since we had been locked out by the owners. With the appeal of some money from *somewhere*, I actually went in to my nearest unemployment office, stood in the depressing line, looked over the forms, and left before my turn came up. I just couldn't force myself to go through the steps of asking for this kind of help. I would make things work some other way.

My "strike weeks" then were spent working out at local fields and whatever weight room would give us access. I played a fair amount of golf with a few other players, out at a club that gave us free access. I got a ladder and many gallons of thick, oil-based stain and stained the entire exterior of our house—a job I swore never to do again. I fretted over the strike, read the news stories back and forth, exchanged rumors with teammates. It was a long and stressful 57 days.

Finally, the owners figured it out: we'll simply "buy" the player votes we need to get a new collective bargaining agreement approved. Called the "Money Now" program (literally, that is what it was called), it was brilliant. The owners basically put together a long-term (5 years) CBA they could live with, put it in front of the NFLPA and players, and "frosted" the cake with cash payments to all current players, which escalated with tenure, at $10,000 a season. So my "money now" was $30,000, while for a 7-year vet it was $70,000, and so on. Remember, the average salary in 1982 was around $90,000, so this was real, hard cash, and for many players it would more than make up for the 57-day strike. For players like me, or rookies, it was a break-even or worse, and the trade, of course, was taking the CBA as offered. Some of us called it the "Money Later" or "Money Never" plan. But it worked brilliantly, and the players voted yes, got their money now, and gave the owners another 5 years of a system that worked very well for the NFL.

The players got some additional benefits, but no revenue sharing, no real loosening of the restrictions on player movement (nothing close to free agency would appear for many years). When all was said and done, for me personally, the strike was basically a financial break-even at the time. The one significant player benefit which was negotiated was a severance payment paid to veterans upon retirement, which I would put to good use at that time.

When we got back to work, the season was abbreviated to 9 total games, so 7 more to make the playoffs. We went on a hot streak and finished 7-2 with a very high seeding in the playoffs. After the strike, I played very little for the rest of the year. Yes, I was still a backup, and on special teams, but my opportunities to play just didn't happen much. We rolled into the playoffs with confidence and swagger. We had a great record and were playing a lower-ranked NY Jets team at home in the first round of our expected trip back to the Super Bowl . . . Or so we thought. The Jets were on fire that day, and put up 44 points on us in a blowout. We staggered out of the stadium to our post-game offensive line party, and just stared at each other. The season was over. No more playoffs, no Super Bowl, no redemption. Unbelievable.

With the off-season suddenly upon us, all our attention turned toward Lauren's birth. Remember, we were 24 years old. There wasn't a lot of "training" for new parents, and our families were far away. Sure, we did the birthing classes, to be ready for the natural birth together experience. But not really any training for what to do with a *newborn*. Oh, well, we were 24, and ignorance was bliss.

As our due date approached, we'd done a couple of ultrasounds (new technology at the time), but couldn't even tell if it was a girl or a boy. The image looked to me like the grainy grayish reception on a bad black-and-white TV. The doctor guessed it was a boy. Boys ran in my family, girls in Cindy's. Our doctor was a big Bengals fan, so we got good attention. Finally, the due date, late January, rolled around. Nothing. No contractions, no water, no action. We took drives, drove over railroad tracks, ate spicy food. Nothing. A week went by. That baby was big and getting bigger. The doctor finally said another week, and if no action, then we'd induce labor. Cindy wanted to go natural, if possible; no drugs.

After the week went by, we checked into the hospital for the inducement of labor. We were warned it would make the contractions and pain more severe. February 2, 1983, in Cincinnati, and a heat wave was hitting the city. It was almost 60 degrees outside, but of course the hospital had the heat on full blast in February, and there was no turning it off. Opening the windows didn't really help. Cindy was sweating and hurting from the very first inducement contraction. And then it got worse. And hotter. And worse.

Hours went by, little progress. The pain got so bad she finally had an epidural. More hours, more contractions, more yelling. Finally, after over 8 hours of this, the doctor decided a C-section was in order.

Thank goodness! Now, this is fairly major surgery, and typically husbands didn't attend a C-section birth. But I told the doctor I wanted to be in the room, with Cindy, when Lauren was born, surgery or not.

I held Cindy's hand during the prep and the incising, and then, yes, walked around where the action was, with the doctor, and my *camera*, to be sure we caught Lauren's first moments. I am sure Cindy would have protested more had she been able, but she was a bit occupied and anesthetized at the time. So in gown and mask I was right there when Lauren was delivered and passed up to Mom right out of the womb. All 10 pounds, 3 ounces of her—good grief! No wonder we had to go C-section! And there it was, I was a father, a dad. Happiest day of my life, becoming a dad. And it has been the best part of my life ever since. And we had a girl! First girl on my side of the family in 3 or 4 generations—cause for celebration.

In those days after a C-section birth Mom and baby spent 2–3 days in the hospital recovering. I visited when I could, including dinners with Cindy and Lauren, this little tiny (remember, I am 6 foot 5, 260 pounds) baby that I am now responsible for. How to hold her? How to carry her? How to change a diaper? Well, we learned fast, mostly by trial and error, fortunately not too much of the latter. We went home as a family for the first time, and our house seemed a lot fuller all of a sudden. And the steady stream of relatives began, mostly helpful (especially my mother-in-law Barb!). And yes, everything changes when you become a parent.

About the time we got fairly situated at home, with the off-season underway, it was time for the NFL draft again. This was always important to me because as a backup offensive lineman, I knew my spot on the roster every year would be a competition. So I wanted to see who they drafted—any offensive linemen and how high in the draft. I remember specifically how I found out about this draft. I was up at the courthouse on one of my paralegal runs and there happened to be a TV on. I saw a quick sports flash that with their first pick in the draft the Bengals had taken Dave Rimington, a center from Nebraska. *A center? And first pick?* We already had an established and good starter in Blair Bush. Where did that leave me? I felt a pit in my stomach. No team carried three centers, and this guy wasn't drafted number one by the Bengals not to play center. I felt my future with the Bengals, and in the NFL, was back to being as uncertain as ever. And for most players, that was, and is, the reality of the game. Competition, injuries, new coaches—any of it could end a career immediately. No warning or discussion.

There was speculation in the media, some of which included my exit. I tried to go through my normal work and workout routines, preparing for training camp. Then, before we opened camp, the second shocker: the Bengals traded Bush to the Seahawks. Trades were very unusual in these days, so that was another very surprising turn of events. And so, just like that, we had two centers again, and I am now the NFL veteran. And while I knew the Bengals first-round pick would be expected to become the starter, I went into camp with the attitude and approach that *I* was the starter and would earn the spot and keep it, even though Rimington was a first-round pick. So, once again, training camp, my fourth, was a battleground. I was in there trying to establish myself as the starter, show that the Bengals should go with my experience. There was no questioning Rimington's athletic prowess—he was a 290-pound block of a man, incredibly powerful. But I'd learned a lot about technique, particularly pass-blocking, that is difficult to master. Plus, I had the advantage of knowing our playbook inside and out.

When the dust settled, I was indeed the starter when the season opened. My line coach made it clear that the new guy would start in time, but he wasn't ready yet. I played my ass off those first few games, and I personally had a good start to the season. But a few games in (it didn't help that we had a bad start 1-4), and not without some grumbling from some of the other linemen, I was told to step aside for the rookie. As frustrating as it was, I did it with good team spirit, coaching him along as ultimately we wanted to win ball games. But inside, I was mad, frustrated, pissed off.

My frustrations were mitigated somewhat by the new ways the

coaches found to use me on the team. Not only was I backing up at center, as well as guard, tackle, and long snapping, our offensive coordinator also threw me into other spots, such as the extra blocking tight end on goal line plays. He even had me line up and split out like a wide receiver in one game, and once I even went in motion as a receiver—not something many #60s get to do in their careers. I never had a pass actually thrown at me as a Bengal, but stay tuned . . .

This season passed slowly and frustratingly, as seven games in, we were 1 win and 6 losses. We had essentially played ourselves out of the playoffs, and after a couple years of being in the Super Bowl hunt, and going once, this kind of record was a huge disappointment. And, I was in the last year of my contract with the Bengals, and there was no real indication they wanted to talk to me about my contract. With the new starter and #1 draft choice in place, they clearly viewed me as a backup, and backups have a short shelf life and a limit on how much they'll get paid. Especially offensive linemen. Even at this stage I figured my time with the Bengals *might* be nearing an end, but I kept that compartmentalized during the season. I even became the Bengals' union player representative. The position didn't mean much, except that I became more knowledgeable about the Collective Bargaining Agreement, and if there were player complaints or concerns I was supposed to address them with management or move the issue up the union chain of command.

Our union at the time was not very strong or well-funded, and the owners tolerated it accordingly. I only recall one issue that came up, something about the way the Bengals were paying us our meal money on road trips. I raised it with the GM Mike Brown, who listened and made the requested adjustment. And, after the season, I did get to take Cindy with me to the annual union meeting in Hawaii—our first time in Hawaii. At the time she was pregnant with Hudson. After our first, we wasted little time going for #2, and were quickly successful.

This pregnancy for Cindy was as tough as the first, but in a different way. Hudson was an active and large baby in utero, and just basically beat Cindy up from the inside out, especially in the last few months. Unlike with Lauren, we had a good ultrasound picture and knew we were having a boy this time. And in those days, the normal medical advice after the first baby was delivered by C-section was that the next would be too. So there was no uncertainty this time around the birth: we scheduled the date, June 4, arrived at the hospital at 8 a.m., and about an hour later, Hudson was born (9 pounds 10 ounces—another big baby!). Easy for the dad, not so easy for Cindy, though avoiding a day of nonproductive labor was a plus.

Again, Cindy's mom spent time with us to help us acclimate to *TWO* kids, but for her it was easy (she'd had five in 6 years). We had also moved in 1983 into a new, larger home, in a beautiful spot with lots of room for our family. But that also meant more stairs and work for Cindy with two small children. And I would be leaving for training camp in about two months, and be gone for a month. Somehow she figured it all out and took care of the kids with some help from me around my workouts and work (I was still part-timing for a law firm). That off-season flew by, with Lauren's first birthday, Hudson's birth, and getting settled in our new house.

On the football front, things were *anything* but settled. First our head coach, Coach Gregg, decided to take the head coaching job at his old team, the Green Bay Packers. The Packers had been in a funk of mediocrity for years under Bart Starr, and Coach Gregg was hired to turn the team around. Second, another spring, another draft. This time, in the ninth round, a center was drafted. Since Rimington, the #1 choice the year before, was firmly in as the starter, this draft selection meant that for me, the current backup center, in the last year of my contract, I had some serious competition for my spot. Especially when combined with a coaching change, even though our line coach was retained.

I went through the off-season training program with my usual rigor—coming in to camp motivated to win my job (two kids, two mortgages—our first house had still not been sold). In great shape, and now 265–270 pounds, I was experienced and ready to play. But I wasn't getting good vibrations from my line coach or management.

My line coach was fuzzy on plans for the newly drafted center . . . and me. Management just ignored the fact that I was in the last year of my contract. Looking back, I should have known what was coming, but you can't let yourself think that way when battling for a job.

At one point in training camp, early, I did speak with my line coach honestly and openly. I told him that if there was going to be a change, that I hoped he would respect me enough to let me go early in training camp so that I'd have a better shot at catching on with another team before the season started. There was little roster movement in the NFL once the season began.

We went into training camp with new head coach Sam Wyche. He was *very* different from Coach Gregg, as you might expect a former QB to differ from a former offensive lineman. Training camp was less intense, more cerebral, less contact. And no nutcracker drill. In a way, it was a nice break from what I was used to. Still, I was fighting for a roster spot, so it was intense enough for me.

In the middle of August and training camp, me at Wilmington, Ohio, sweating away, Cindy at home with two small babies working away, we received tragic news. Cindy's younger brother, who was also then a student at the College of Wooster, was killed in a grain truck accident while working his summer job. He was actually making his last truck run of the summer before going home, and then back to Wooster. And the truck went off the road. And here, in hindsight, I made a decision I still regret to this day. After talking it over with Cindy, I stayed in training camp, rather than taking a few days off to go to Doug's service in Minnesota. I felt my job was on the line, and that I simply couldn't leave camp. A family, two house payments—I had to stay and make the team. Cindy and her parents understood. But I should have gone, should have been there. Even now, over 25 years later, this hurts me to write. I did what I thought was "right" at the time, but it wasn't. Cindy attended Doug's service—I stayed in Wilmington and practiced.

After we broke camp, the final roster cuts were coming up. The numbers said that another offensive lineman had to go. We still had three centers, not really workable. When I walked into Spinney Field, the last day I'd be there as a Bengal, I shouldn't have been shocked, but I still was. Before I even made it to the locker room, I was steered into a side room. There, GM Mike Brown had a piece of paper for me to sign, a "waiver slip," which basically was my termination slip. The Bengals fired me. I was stunned and wandered in to clear out my locker, say a few good-byes. I kept up a brave front, but inside I was writhing, in turmoil. What to tell Cindy? What to tell my parents and friends? How to pay the bills, support my family? All this ran through my head over and over that morning. I reminded my line coach that I'd asked him not to wait until the last cut to fire me—but business is business. They had done what was best for the Bengals. And this, certainly, is when you know the NFL is a business.

I was out of Spinney Field, and the Bengals world, in less than an hour. A "free agent" (read: unemployed), with the season starting in a week and teams finalizing their rosters, cutting the last few players to make it to 45. I was now one of those: a casualty, a free agent, a backup offensive lineman looking for a spot with any other team. Too late to start law school this year, and without the money to do it anyway, I had to figure out what was next. Was I done in the NFL? I wasn't ready to be done, knew I could play if given the chance. So I resolved to try to work my way onto another team. And as soon as possible.

CHAPTER 6

The Green Bay Packers (1984–1986)

LET'S RESET THE picture here. We had two children under age two. We lived in a nice house with a large (at the time) mortgage of over $100,000. We still owned our first home, with a mortgage of around $70,000. Both with interest rates in the 12%–13% range (remember the mid-'80s? High inflation?). Cindy was in the middle of getting her MBA and taking care of our new family and household—a full-time job in and of itself. We had some savings, but only a few thousand dollars. I was unemployed, from a profession where there are *very few* openings. Were we stressed? Yes. Worried? Yes. But also young and optimistic that with work and effort it would all work out.

Somehow.

I had never had an agent before, but decided I needed someone to help "market" me to other teams. On the recommendation of my former teammate Dan Ross, I hired his agent to represent me in trying to catch on with another team. He also had contacts with the newly formed USFL, a competitor league with the NFL (soon to be crushed, like all other NFL competitors), as well as with all the NFL teams. I started visiting teams that had a potential need for a backup offensive lineman, with experience, and importantly, long-snapping skills. I visited the Pittsburgh Steelers, Indianapolis Colts, and Green Bay Packers. Each team had me run through a different screening process, sometimes with a workout demonstration of long-snapping skills and other drills. After each visit, the team representative would thank me for my time and say they'd be in touch. This all happened over the course of the first two weeks of the season. Each week that went by was another week without a game check. I watched the games on TV, but it sure was hard.

After my visit to the Colts I thought that might be my spot. They needed an experienced backup, and I thought I worked out well for them. In the meantime, my agent was working on a possible deal with the USFL Pittsburg Maulers. The Packers, where my former head coach Forrest Gregg was now the head coach, were also still interested. But "still interested" wasn't paying any bills. My agent finally called me to say the Packers were serious. "Pack your bags and go to Green Bay to sign and become a Green Bay Packer." I was excited and relieved and nervous. Excited to be going to an NFL team coached by someone I knew, relieved that I'd found a job for another season, and nervous that I'd be with a new team, and I wouldn't know a single person there, except Coach Gregg. I knew I was going to have to prove myself all over again, with the Packers, and right in the middle of the season.

I flew to Green Bay and checked into the official Packers hotel—I think it was a Ramada or a Sheraton. This would be my home, a hotel room, until Cindy and the kids could make it up to Green Bay and join me. Like my first training camp in Wilmington, Ohio, in 1980, I was alone in a strange city, no friends, no contacts, no context, except that I was there to prove my worth as a lineman for the Packers.

First day there I went over to the Packers facility and knew this would be different than my Bengals experience—and better! The practice facilities, the locker room, the training room, the weight room—were all very different from what I had been used to at Cincinnati's Spinney Field. When I walked in the door, every day, I walked past the trophy case of Super Bowl trophies, Hall of Fame players, NFL championships, Vince Lombardi everywhere. Into the players' locker room which seemed to be twice the size of our locker room in Cincinnati, with a giant Green Bay Packers logo in the carpet in the middle of the room. Here, when I needed equipment or different shoes or *anything*, all I had to do was ask.

My contract with the Packers was a *raise* from when I was with the Bengals. I signed a 2-year deal for $120,000 for the '84 season, and $140,000 for the next year (of course, I had to make the team to get that). I had just gotten a 50 percent raise by being fired by the Bengals, and landed at a team that treated its players like they were a treasure. The practice facilities were actually at and adjacent to the stadium, fabled Lambeau Field, which, for a football player, is an unbelievable place to play (more later). The stadium and facilities are located on Lombardi Avenue, of course. All in a metropolitan area of about 150,000 people, but people with a passion for their Packers that was unlike anything I'd ever seen. I was going to love it here in Green Bay.

Now, there was a reason Coach Gregg had been brought in to replace another Green Bay legend—Bart Starr. The team had struggled for years, with only one playoff trip in Bart Starr's 9-year tenure. And Coach Gregg's job was to change this . . . and do it fast. He had a very different coaching philosophy from his predecessor, the difference you'd expect between a quarterback (Starr) and offensive lineman (Gregg). Coach Gregg was no-nonsense, intense, competitive, uncompromising, hit-the-other-team-in-the-mouth tough. And he expected every player on his team to be the same. I knew this from having played for Coach Gregg for four years—in fact it was *the only* way I knew in the NFL. But the team Coach Gregg inherited was used to a very different style, and I realized that when I first got there and started hearing the stories of the incredibly tough training camp, the hard, full-contact practices, the conditioning drills that the team had gone through with Coach Gregg that summer. All things I was used to. And, I am sure, part of the reason Coach Gregg brought me to Green Bay. In me he had a believer, a player who shared his approach and had seen it work all the way to the Super Bowl. He needed more attitudes like mine, and I came willing to bring that attitude.

Of course, that could make the situation with my teammates

challenging. First, I was "the new guy ," had not been through training camp with them, and was not a superstar. For some, I am sure I
represented a threat to their group, which had played together for
a while. I was not brought in to start right away, but to back up the
longtime veteran center, a smallish center for the day (6 foot 0, 255
pounds), but who was very experienced and had great technique. He
was a 10-year vet, one of those players who has held the spot so long
that it is hard to think of anyone else playing there. My signing was a
shot across the bow that status quo was not protected.

While not signed to start immediately, I knew from talking with
Coach Gregg and the line coach that I'd have a shot to move into the
starting lineup. This all made for pretty tense dynamics with my fellow offensive linemen and others on the team. They grumbled a lot
about Coach Gregg and his approach. I embraced it and told people
how it could pay off in wins and playoffs—but yes, it was hard. This
change in attitude is hard to accomplish in one season.

In Cincinnati, Coach Gregg had a different group of players and
team leaders who were willing to buy into his philosophy, even
though that first year was also a challenge. In Green Bay, there was a
different dynamic among the players, as if Coach Gregg had to prove
to them that his way was a winning way. Many players liked the "old
way"—it was easier, practices not so bad, going 8-8 wasn't terrible,
and hey, they all collected a paycheck. The Coach Gregg way was
tough, uncompromising, and it would take some time before it would
pay dividends.

I often think Coach Gregg's biggest mistake in Green Bay was
not making the decision to clear out all the naysayers in his first year,
even though some of them were "stars" of the team. The negativity, I
think, proved to be just enough to prevent the *team* commitment to
Coach Gregg's approach that I believe would have generated a different result. I am sure others had a different perspective.

My first few weeks in Green Bay were a whirlwind. We were
already three games into the season and 1-2 when I got there. I was
handed a thick playbook, equipment, and had to learn a new system

as well as a whole new group of players. I had a few days of practice, and then we were on the plane to Dallas, where I would dress for the game but only play in an emergency.

We got beaten, and in my first trip to the old Cowboys Stadium I was struck by one oddity: as I stood on one sideline looking across the field to the other sideline, I couldn't see the feet of the other players there—the field was "crowned" so severely in the middle that the slope was that noticeable. Very strange—didn't notice that on any other field I played on. Anyway, we lost, and lost, and lost. After winning the first game, the Packers lost 7 straight. Some were close, some not, some memorable. Like our Monday night game in Denver (remember, my first pro football game was in Denver, in 1980), where we played through a freak snowstorm on October 15 on Monday Night Football. Lynn Dickey, our QB, had an amazing game in the snow and threw for over 300 yards (very unusual in those days), but we still managed to lose.

Coach Gregg was beside himself. One win, seven losses . . . *in a row?* Things had to change. After the Denver loss (1-6), and yet another dismal performance by our field goal kicker (0 for 2), Coach Gregg couldn't take it anymore. In the middle of our Monday film session, after watching our kicker miss his second attempt (we lost the game by 3 points), he slammed down the remote control. "You are our kicker! All you have to do is go out there and kick the damn ball through the uprights. *That's* why you're here, why we pay you. Well, you couldn't even kick my ass!" Now, we couldn't laugh out loud in the meeting. But the comment, coming from Coach Gregg, who had a typically large offensive lineman's butt, was actually pointed, and hysterical. Our kicker was gone that day, replaced by a rookie, but that line to a kicker "you couldn't kick my ass!" lived on for the rest of the season. A classic Forrest Gregg moment, and another chapter in Coach Gregg's "challenged" relationship with kickers in general.

Shortly after I signed my contract in Green Bay, I found a house to rent and moved out of the team hotel. Cindy and the kids, with a driving assist from her father, piled into the Volvo with as many personal belongings as they could stuff into the car around the car seats. After driving most of the night, they arrived at our mostly empty rental house, 3 bedrooms, 2½ baths in a nice little neighborhood a 10-minute drive from Lambeau Field. Of course, most places in Green Bay are a 10-minute drive from Lambeau Field. Being the middle of the season already, Cindy (as usual) did most of the setting up at home. Between practice, games, and travel, I was barely around. But Green Bay is a small town, we had lovely neighbors, and everyone loved (and knew!) the Packers—even if we weren't winning. Green Bay was (is!) a wonderful slice of Midwest life. Especially during football season, all life seemed to revolve around the Packers. Of course, every home game Sunday there were about 60,000 fans at the game, and more tailgating in the parking lot—in a metro area of about 150,000 total!!

There are only two seasons in Green Bay—Football/Packer season and "other." When moving to a new city, I usually have a moment when I realize "Hey, I really am in a new place!" For me, it happened one fall morning on the drive into practice. Still waking up, I was sitting at a stoplight (there aren't many) when I noticed something odd about the car ahead of me. Something was strapped to the top of the car, and as I stared at it a while, I realized the glassy eye of a deer was staring back at me. Yes, deer season had begun! Then that following Sunday at the game in Lambeau, I noticed many fans there in camouflage gear and bright orange reflector vests—apparently they had come straight to the game from their weekend hunt to cheer for their beloved Packers.

At home games, I arrived at the stadium at around 9 or so for a noon kickoff (Central Time Zone). Already, at that hour, the parking lot was more than half full, with trucks and cars and grills and smoke and beer everywhere. The smell of brats and onions cooking over any heating device available filled the air—and yes, I was ready for a brat at that hour of the day! Fans were laughing and yelling encouragement at any player that came into view.

Across Lombardi Avenue, the white picket fence had been

repainted green and gold, with a "Welcome Back Forrest" painted along it as well. All this excitement and enthusiasm, and we were in the middle of a *bad* losing streak. And inside the stadium? Even better. No luxury boxes. No padded seats. Old-school aluminum-style benches from the field level to the top. And all full—every Sunday— every season. Fans who loved the game and their Packers. Fans for whom, even in a tough season, the next NFL championship, the next Super Bowl, had to be just a few games away.

In this season of mediocrity in Green Bay, there were a few games and events that really stood out for me as a player. We played the Chicago Bears twice a year as division opponents. And at that time Walter Payton was the Bears' featured running back, and he was in his prime. To watch him run the ball, move, sidestep, accelerate, punish tacklers, score—he was one of a kind. And I was watching him work only a few steps away.

I also remember well the game we turned our losing streak around. We were 1-7, losers of 7 in a row, and were hosting Detroit in Green Bay. Our division rival Lions, at home. Though we'd been losing, the losses were close. There was a sense that we were ready to break out, and there would be no place like home, at Lambeau, to make that happen. A perfect October day for football. We took an early lead of 14-3 in the first quarter, then 21-6 in the second. My playing time thus far had been mostly on special teams, and also as the "extra" tight end on short yardage and goal line situations. In other words, if we had 1 or 2 or 3 yards to go for a first down or a touchdown, we would send in our "big" package. I would report in as an eligible receiver (as #60, my number made me ineligible to line up as a receiver or tight end unless I reported into a referee as "eligible"—then I could line up as an eligible receiver, block, catch a pass, etc.), and then serve as an extra 270-pound blocker as a tight end to help pave the way for our running back to plow into the line for a couple of yards.

I got used to the unusual tight end spot and my blocking assignments, and liked it. When I was in as the extra tight end, we almost always ran the ball, and I blocked. Almost always. Toward the end of the second quarter, leading 21-9, we had the ball down at the Lions' 3 yard line, 3rd down and goal. I was in as the extra tight end, and normally we'd call a running play and try to jam the ball across the goal line—especially since Coach Gregg, as a former offensive lineman, preferred to run it in.

The play came into the huddle. I had remembered to report in as an "eligible" receiver. The play was a play-action pass, designed to go to one of our regular tight ends. My job on the play was to block hard, as if it was a run, and then turn around as the *third* option for our QB Dickey. As the third option down on the goal line, there was no way I'd see a pass because the play happened too fast down there with only 3 yards to go.

Dickey yelled out the count, I fired out into my defender, blocking him hard for a one count, two count, three count, then I turned back to act like the third option as receiver. Well, the first option, our tight end, forgot what he was supposed to do. That's right, forgot (it happens). The number 2 option was, apparently, covered. As the third option—me—turned to look back at the QB to see the play finish up after my decoy block, the ball came whistling at my head in a tight spiral. I barely had time to react as it hit me right under my chin, and I instinctively grabbed at the ball with my hands, almost in self-defense, falling to the turf in the end zone. I heard the crowd roar.

The whistle blew, the referee had his arms up over his head. *Touchdown!* Holy shit, I had caught a touchdown pass! I'd never imagined such a thing could happen. I lumbered to my feet, looked around briefly, and then did what I knew I had to do—gave that ball a huge atomic spike into the end zone while the Lambeau crowd went wild and my teammates slapped me on the back. We kicked the extra point, and as I jogged over to the sideline, Coach Gregg was, quite uncharacteristically, laughing on the sideline—he couldn't believe it! Neither could I!

Cindy, who was up in the player wives' section at the game, heard the roar of the crowd but was talking to someone and had to ask what happened. "Your husband scored a touchdown!" someone yelled. To which Cindy replied, "No, he's a center, he never scores." Very funny. But finally they convinced her. That touchdown put us up 28-9, and we never looked back and demolished the Lions that day. After the game, I was interviewed by press and TV alike, asking me about the play and what it felt like to score my first NFL touchdown. I told them I was as surprised as they were, and was glad Dickey was so accurate that he basically wedged the ball in under my face mask—almost impossible to drop. What a fun day that was. And yes, I did retrieve the ball, and it sits safely in my trophy case. If you look back at the cover of this book, that is the TD catch.

The next game that stands out in that season was also against the Lions, a few weeks later, on Thanksgiving Day in Detroit in the Silverdome. The line coach had decided that I would start this game. I was excited to be starting—not my first start in the NFL, but my first start as a Green Bay Packer. And I'd be playing on Thanksgiving Day, nationally televised, and all my friends and family would be watching the kid from the College of Wooster playing the Lions. We had just thrashed the Lions a few weeks ago and went into the game very confident.

The first quarter we roared out, looking for our fifth win in a row after our horrible start. At 5-7 we were still in the playoff race. We jumped to a 14-0 lead in the first quarter. I remember later my mom told me that we made it look so easy she turned off the game to have Thanksgiving dinner with her family. When she came back to the TV, at the end of the third quarter, the Lions had come back and were now *beating us* 24-21. Then they went up 31-21. I was playing well at center, having a good game personally, but that wasn't enough. We made it close, 28-31, but lost the game. The locker room was quiet. My good individual effort was little solace when the team lost. We changed and took the short flight back to Green Bay.

Once back, we couldn't go home to lick our wounds. Oh no. We had a previously arranged team Thanksgiving dinner, attendance required for all players and families, with Coach Gregg and other coaches. While a nice idea, tough to do after a loss like that. We tried to be thankful. Our little girl, Lauren, almost two years old with red-haired pigtails flying, was innocently immune to the somber attitude in the room. For her, it was a party. And she kept wandering over to stare at Coach Gregg, who would do his best to stare back but couldn't help but break into a smile and laugh at this audacious toddler.

The other reason I remember this game, even today, is because of the way the rest of the season played out. We had three games left and were 5-8. I was the starting center for the rest of the season, having acquitted myself well in the Detroit game. We hosted Tampa Bay the next week, and after falling behind 14-0, we came back and beat them 27-14. Then, the next week we were in Chicago, against the 9-5 Bears. The Bears were leading our division and wanted to seal their playoff position with a win. They played an amazingly tough and aggressive defense, coached by defensive legend Buddy Ryan. Four good defensive linemen, fast linebackers, on a cold (wind chill 24) day on the frozen turf at Soldier Field. And the Packer-Bear rivalry was as cold and bitter as they come.

We went in with our backup QB, Dickey out hurt. It was a slug fest. We beat on each other for 3 hours. The turf was hard as rock. I remember after this game I was sore until the following Thursday. Walter Payton rushed for 175 yards. Their defense just kept coming. But we refused to give in and held a 7-0 lead going in at halftime. I'm sure we got one of Coach Gregg's classic halftime speeches about desire and finishing the job. The 3rd quarter ended with us up 13-7, and then in the 4th, the Bears scored to make it 14-13.

It would have been easy to fold then. It was frigidly cold, the crowd was screaming, the defense was rushing our QB like demons, but we fought back, refused to give in. With a long touchdown pass, we took the lead and the game 20-13. I remember it as one of my most satisfying moments as an NFL player: we won, against a good team, in harsh conditions, and I got to start and lead as center. It is hard to describe the feeling that comes with a win like that—the emotion, the satisfaction, the accomplishment. It is why I played the game.

We finished our season at Minnesota, another division rival, in the Metrodome. While we knew then we were out of the playoffs, we also wanted to finish strong with a win, and go 8-8 for the season. My in-laws, Phil and Barb, who had been Vikings fans for the better part of 40 years, came down to see the game, putting them in the awkward position of rooting for the Packers and their son-in-law. At least, they told me they did. We came out strong and never let up, whipping the Vikings at home, 38-14, and getting our seventh win in 8 games. The second half of the season was great, great to be a Packer and winning! And for the last four games I started and played well, leaving me with high expectations for the next season.

Recall that Thanksgiving Day loss to the Lions, a game that we had, and then gave away? As it turns out, had we won that game, we were 9-7 and would have made the playoffs as a wild card. Who knows how far we could have gone—playing well and together as a team. I still sting from that loss, and the lost opportunity, to this day.

And just like that, my first year in Green Bay, and fifth year in the NFL, was over. We packed up our stuff, loading up two cars for the trip back to Cincinnati. Given the circumstances of the move to Green Bay, we'd never had time to think of it as anything but "temporary." We still had our home in Cincinnati, where we lived, and the first home we were still trying to sell, which was currently leased. So we headed back to Cincinnati to assess our lives and future.

Cindy was still working on her MBA. The diversion to Green Bay, along with Hudson's birth, had not been very conducive to her studies. One good reason to return to Cincinnati was for Cindy to continue classes at Xavier. Another was that I could continue working with the law firm where I'd been spending time clerking. And, finally, it was as much of a home as we had, even though we realized our main reason for being there—the Cincinnati Bengals—was finished. Cindy got back into MBA classes, I got back to work and off-season workouts.

Lauren turned 2 in February. My schedule allowed enough flexibility that I could help with the kids a fair amount, allowing Cindy time for classes and study. But through all this we knew that our future was not in Cincinnati. Rather, we knew that, at least for the 1985 football season, I would be heading back to Green Bay, very optimistic of my chances not just to make the team, but to start. So, we decided to put our home on Burney Lane on the market.

We were nervous about selling. Our prior experience, trying to sell our first home, had been a disaster. In fact, after more than two years, it still wasn't sold. We were still making those monthly payments, on a 13¾ percent mortgage, just barely covered by the rent we were getting. So when we put our Burney Lane house on the market, we weren't sure what to expect.

We had improved the house since we bought it for $115,000 in 1983. Paint, finishings and furnishings, and some landscaping work. One hot weekend the prior summer I had spent hours with a pickax and shovel in rock-hard ground, planting some shrubbery that we hoped would grow up and give a little more privacy from the road that ran near our house. Seemed like a good idea, and I pounded and sweated and blistered several shrub plants into the unyielding turf—really, it was rock with a little dirt mixed in. But I got the damn things planted and watered them for the next couple weeks until small green shoots started appearing. They were alive! Then one afternoon, sitting out on our deck, I heard a noise slowly approaching down the road. It was a big public works roadside mower, and as it came down the road I realized—to my horror—what was about to happen. Without pausing, the machine buzz-cut right over my tender plants, reducing them to splintered stubs. I just stared.

Well, back to our story. We put the place on the market for about $135,000, given prices had gone up in our neighborhood over the time we'd been in the house. We had some interested parties, and finally a contract with a couple who told us they would pay cash for the home. *Cash?* We couldn't imagine someone having that much cash, but it sounded good to us. We got all the documents ready for closing.

Now, financial historians will recall that in early 1984 the U.S. was going through a very challenging economic time, and one crisis that was about to erupt was the Savings and Loan financial institutions crisis. Many of these institutions were going, or were about to go, broke. And our buyers, it turned out, had much of the cash they needed for the purchase sitting in one of those threatened S&Ls. As we heard the story, they got in line at their local branch to get their money out—along with many others in a long line to take all *their* money out. Literally, a run on the bank.

They came to the closing of our house sale, attended by Cindy, with a brown paper bag full of cash that they'd managed to get out of their account a day or two before their S&L shut down. *Wow*. We closed the deal, happily, and then moved to a little rental home we'd found on Grandle Court, about a fourth the size of our house. We crammed all our belongings into the one-story cottage and garage, not really knowing how long we'd be there. And that is one of the ironies of my NFL life. I'd played for 5 years, had just had my most lucrative season, sold our house for a profit . . . and here we were renting an old, small bungalow in a Cincinnati suburb, having no idea how long we'd be there or where we'd live next. We assumed it would be Green Bay, but we couldn't plan on Green Bay until I had made the team in August, and even then, what would that mean? Another year, another season . . . and then what? The uncertainty, the transient nature of our lives with a young family was beginning to wear on us.

This uncertainty— being cut, no income, not sure what the NFL future would bring—led to some pretty serious discussions about my future and law school. Duke had given me an open-ended deferral. Cindy, at some point, had another idea—she suggested I apply to Harvard Law School. Now, since I had been rejected by both Stanford and Michigan during my initial application process in 1980, I was skeptical Harvard would be any different. But Cindy reasoned that my NFL experience would make me stand out from all the other applicants with good grades and scores. She was right—I applied . . . and was accepted. We flew to Harvard to meet with the Dean of

Admissions, and also to ask for a deferral because I planned to play for the Packers in 1985. No problem, said Harvard. Now, I had two great options for law school.

Notwithstanding the seemingly transient nature of our lives, from a football standpoint, I was as optimistic as ever. I finished the season as the veteran starter for the Packers. Rumor was that their longtime center would retire. That would leave me, and a rookie from 1984, as the incumbents at the center spot, and me as the starter.

I was training in Cincinnati, and as a *former* Bengal, that meant I was on my own for working out. No coaching and no Bengal facilities. And in these days, there were not nice gyms in every neighborhood available for a serious weight lifter. Luckily, my old strength coach, who had personally trained and coached me for four years in Cincinnati, had an office at a hotel in Cincinnati. He was a part owner of the old Nautilus line of strength training equipment, and in the hotel, in a private area, he had set up a fully equipped workout room, complete with bench press, a full line of brand-new Nautilus machines, and a juke box to crank the tunes. He gave me a key, and after my half days of work at the law firm, I would go to the workout room, called the Kong Room (King Kong), and push myself to the limit. It was just me alone, forcing myself to do one more repetition, add another 5 or 10 pounds, do another set until my muscles screamed.

After about an hour of that, I'd drag myself out on the street to do 1–2 miles of road work. And those were strength training days, three times a week, without fail. On the other three days, I would go over to the local high school track, Anderson High School. It was a classic old cinder track circling a football field with white goal posts. Three days a week I'd go there and do my running/speed/endurance workouts, again, alone, with only myself to push. Some days it was so hot and dry that the dust from the cinder track would cling to my body and sweat would run tracks through it down my chest and legs.

I knew I'd have a Coach Gregg training camp, so each running workout would include 2–3 sets of the dreaded grass drills, or up/downs. I'd jog in place, tell myself "Front!" "Up!" "Front!" "Up!"

imagining Coach Gregg yelling the dreaded words during training camp. I knew what I had to do to be ready. By the end of the summer, there were spots on the tough grass of the high school field that were worn bare from my grass drills and hundreds of repetitions, wearing out the grass.

My days at the high school also included working on my long-snapping skills. Now, again, I was there alone, so no one to actually snap the ball *to*. What to do? I'd had the Packers send me a bag of footballs that I would take with me to the field. After my running drills, I'd get the balls out, pace off the right distance from the goal post (15 yards for punts, 7 yards for kicks), and then use the goal post as my "kicker/punter," trying to zip the ball through my legs with a perfect spiral and hit the goal post. Not easy, but part of my regular routine.

By the end of summer, I had my weight pushing 275 pounds, my heaviest, but yet I felt I was stronger than ever, and in the best physical condition I'd ever been in. Under my new Green Bay Packers strength coach, the conditioning test at camp would be a series of 4 x 400-yard runs, with specified times for each position to achieve. If you didn't make the times, you had to keep re-testing during training camp until passing. No way I was doing this more than once, and for the last few weeks of training the summer of 1985, I'd set up and "run the test" until I was confident I could do it. Running a series of 400-yard runs at a pace that approached 70%–80% of a sprint, for a 275-pound offensive lineman, with only about 75 seconds rest between each one, was one of the hardest conditioning drills I'd ever done. And there was no faking this test—if you weren't in top shape, you didn't pass.

The hot Cincinnati summer passed by. Hudson turned 1; Lauren was almost 3. I packed for training camp, which was held at St. Norbert College in Green Bay. Though we felt good about my chances to make the team and be in Green Bay, we couldn't pack everything up and move the kids up until I had made it through training camp. Even though I was the incumbent starter, I knew from hard experience to take nothing for granted in the NFL. So I packed up my SUV with training camp gear and drove off to Green Bay to make the team, leaving Cindy alone with two toddlers for a month at least, uncertain, apprehensive, and unsettled.

Training camp in Green Bay was quite a different experience from Cincinnati. Whereas Wilmington—Bengals camp—was an hour outside of Cincinnati, we Packers bunked at St. Norbert College but every day bussed or drove over to the regular Packers training facilities at Lambeau Field. On the first day of camp, coming out of the locker room to walk the 200 yards across the parking lot to our practice field, we were greeted by a group of kids, mostly young boys, waiting there with their bikes. They had all ridden over from their homes to see their Packers, and, if lucky, successfully volunteer to carry a player's helmet and shoulder pads over to the practice field, with the player often riding the kid's bike over. What a cool tradition! Usually you'd end up with a "regular" kid who would be your personal Sherpa for the duration of camp. A thrill for the kids, and players too. It was rather funny to see giant NFL players straddling small bikes, some with "banana" seats and handlebar streamers, wobbling across the parking lot to practice. Probably the riskiest part of practice! The kids would usually be there after practice to help us back, and after a 2-hour Coach Gregg practice, that was certainly appreciated. This would go on until they had to start school, and I think the tradition continues today.

I had some notable teammates in Green Bay, as I did in Cincinnati. James Lofton, one of the best wide receivers to play the game and a future Hall of Famer, was in his prime. Looking over the roster, we had only one 300-pounder. Compare that to today's linemen. This was also the first time I'd ever had a teammate who came to practice for several weeks involved in some kind of treatment program. He was allowed to attend practice, then back to the facility at night. Fortunately, he was finished before our first road game.

Halfway through the season, we added another offensive lineman named Blake—what are the odds that there would be two Blakes, both offensive linemen, on the same NFL team, at the same time? And my hotel roommate for the season was a great guy who came down from the CFL having won four Grey Cup championship rings with the CFL Edmonton Eskimos (he played there with NFL Hall of Famer Warren Moon). His four Grey Cup rings, worn simultaneously, were pretty impressive.

And then there was another teammate who was a self-proclaimed ladies' man, and some of us started to grill him about the wisdom of that, given the odds he'd end up with multiple children and paternity suits if he continued that behavior. He stopped our queries dead in their tracks by proclaiming that his agent had helped him procure "paternity insurance" to protect against this very issue, leaving him free to roam with insured impunity. I can only imagine the insurance application questions. And answers.

Forrest Gregg training camp in Green Bay was not all that different from Forrest Gregg training camp in Wilmington, Ohio. We stayed in a small college dormitory, ate there, and shuttled back and forth to our two-a-day practices. I passed the dreaded conditioning test the first time through, no problem, as I expected to do after my summer of training. Some didn't pass, and watching them fall out after the third or fourth 400-yard run, hands on knees, was painful, especially knowing they'd have to do it again.

As usual, we put on the pads from day one, twice a day, and went full speed, full contact in drills and practice. The first 10 days of camp were the toughest, always, for we would do two 2-hour practices for 10 days in a row, full contact, until our "break" for the first intrasquad scrimmage. That meant bruises, sprains, gashes, tired muscles, headaches, exhaustion, extreme daily weight fluctuations, and endless meetings.

I came into this camp as the first-team center. My competition was a second-year "kid." I was determined to hold my spot and start for the Packers and felt I had a great chance to do it. While we were fairly evenly matched physically/athletically, the other center was a better run blocker, while I was more experienced and a better pass blocker. Pass blocking required more line calls and "on-the-move adjustments," and my years of play gave me an edge here. As did my size, as I was taller with longer arms, which was an asset for pass blocking in the NFL.

We had a good battle going in camp for the starting spot. A week or so in, in a random full-speed drill, someone's helmet struck me flush on my thigh, and it hurt like hell. I limped back to the huddle, trying to shake it off. It was like my quadriceps was semi-paralyzed. I couldn't push off explosively with my right leg. It didn't hurt me on pass blocking, or running generally, but the power I needed to run block was not there. Now, in my position, and in this day, this was one of those injuries you just played through. Going into the training room, missing practice time, was a sure way for me to lose the starting spot. So I gutted it out, but I simply couldn't generate the power I needed. This showed on film when we reviewed the intrasquad scrimmage. I pass blocked well, but just couldn't execute on the running plays.

The other center, though, had the explosiveness the team was looking for on the running game. We both long-snapped on punts and kicks, so the coaches had to make a decision. My line coach finally sat me down and told me that they were going to start the younger guy, that he was the better run blocker and that is what they wanted in the starter. I was crushed but couldn't show it. Then he told me that I'd be used a lot, even regularly, on passing downs because of my experience and superior pass-blocking technique. I had to swallow hard, and then accept the decision and move on. On the plus side, it looked like I would be on the team, with a significant role—I just wouldn't achieve my goal of starting for the year.

I adapted my expectations, and focused my energy on getting even better as a pass blocker, since that would be my "specialty." I would also be playing on special teams and rotate in as the extra big blocking tight end on short yardage situations. So I was going to get a lot of playing time. Still, not starting was a bitter pill to swallow.

Again.

Preseason passed. We found a nice 4-bedroom house in a leafy "suburb" of Green Bay to rent for the season. We gave up the temporary cottage on Grandle Court, in Cincinnati, where Cindy and the kids had been camping, waiting for the final roster moves in Green Bay to be sure that I would make the team, and then they could move up and join me. This time, all our stuff came up to Green Bay—our official departure from Cincinnati. We knew our "home" would be Green Bay for as long as that lasted, and then either a year or two or more later, we would be off to Harvard and law school for me. For even though I was now entering my sixth year as a pro, we understood the future was not football—not long term, anyway. As Paul Brown had said so many years ago to us in training camp—football is a means to an end, not an end in itself. We got settled into our Green Bay house, and the season started with a trip to New England, to play the Patriots.

This was a strange start to the season for me for three reasons. First, though my sixth year in the league, I had never been to New England or played the Patriots—first time to Sullivan Stadium (precursor to Foxborough). Second, this would be my first game where I was the designated pass-blocking center. On third and long, generally I would get the call to go into the game. I spent most of the game very close to Coach Gregg and our offensive coordinator. When they wanted me in, they'd grab me, bark the play at me, and I'd sprint into the huddle with the play for our QB, relaying to him the call I'd just heard, then taking my spot in the huddle to get the play and lead the offense up to the line. I'd review the defense, call out our pass-blocking assignments or blitz calls, if there were any, then snap the ball. After the play, we'd switch again. It worked pretty well, except we got behind and played the whole game that way. A pretty dismal performance all-round.

The third reason this game was strange was the "small world" story. On the other sideline, still dominant in his fourteenth season, eventually headed for the Hall of Fame, was John Hannah—fellow

Baylor High School grad. We didn't exchange any pleasantries before or after the game, and since he was an offensive lineman like me, we weren't on the field at the same time. But I do remember watching him in warm-ups, seeing those giant tree-trunk calves and thighs, and the ferocity in his every move, and I flashed back to when I saw him when I was a skinny kid at Baylor. He scared me then, and he scared me now!

It was a short flight home to Green Bay, but it was a long flight. Winning flights were always short, losing flights were always long. On winning flights there was chatter, laughter, the one or two beers for each player were happily consumed along with the sandwiches and snacks. We all looked forward to watching film the next day. On losing flights, it was quiet. Ice packs were handed out. Stat sheets were passed among coaches. Any rare outburst of laughter was usually answered by Coach Gregg turning to glare at the player who thought *anything* was funny after a loss. We all dreaded watching film the next day, wondering how many times we'd be called out individually for failure. On landing, we'd quickly scatter for home, and 10 or 12 hours later, gather for weight lifting, stretching, and the film session.

Our second game of the year would be memorable because we were playing the New York Giants. The Giants had a player named Lawrence Taylor, who was redefining the outside linebacker position in only his fifth year in the league. As we prepared for the Giants that week, I'd never seen an offensive game plan so centered on a *defensive* player. While common to build a defensive game plan to stop or contain an offensive star, like a Walter Payton or Joe Montana, it was quite unusual to do so for a defensive player. But we put in plays and blocking schemes that were specifically designed to stop, or slow down, Lawrence Taylor. All week the pressure was put squarely on the offensive line—protect our QB—block Lawrence Taylor!

And we did. Though it wasn't a perfect performance, Taylor only got to our QB one time. We took a 10-0 lead in the first quarter, then battled back and forth until we fell behind 20-17 in the fourth quarter, after two touchdown drives by the Giants. We responded, though, and scored the final touchdown to beat a very good Giants team, in Green Bay. The home crowd loved it, and the entire offensive line was awarded a game ball for the win, and our work against one of the best ever—Lawrence Taylor.

Even though Coach Gregg was an "old-school" coach, that didn't mean he was opposed to trying new things. Our starting QB was still Lynn Dickey, and he was known as a very good passer, but he was *not* very mobile at this stage of his career. Think statue. He sported double knee braces after some pretty serious knee injuries during his career, and simply couldn't move around much in the pocket. The shotgun formation, where the QB lines up about 5 yards behind the center, was used in the NFL, but not by many teams. The Dallas Cowboys had used it since the mid-'70s, with Roger Staubach. In this formation, the center snaps the ball back the 5 yards to the QB, so on passing plays, the QB could get the ball and be set up quicker to read the defense and make his decisions. For a less mobile QB, like Dickey, it was even more of an advantage, as he didn't have to sprint back 5–7 yards *after* the snap to then set up and throw—he got the ball and was already there.

Why was this important to me? Well, the shotgun snap is a very different technique for a center than the ordinary direct snap. With the latter, the center basically, with one hand, slams the ball up and into the QB's hands, which are right on his butt. It is a direct handoff, requiring little finesse. However, the shotgun snap is very different. Here, the center must snap the ball back through the air to the QB, about 5 yards, and hit the QB generally from knees to head level. Without looking. In other words, it is a blind snap, because as soon as the snap goes, the center must immediately block, often with a nose tackle a few inches from his face. Balance is key, because too much weight forward will send the ball flying *over* the QB's head. Release the ball too soon, and it will *roll* back toward the QB. Too hard, and the QB might not be able to handle the snap. Coach Gregg wanted to use the shotgun on passing plays, and I was the pass-blocking center.

So, it was my job to learn the shotgun snap.

And, literally, I had to teach myself, through practice (*a lot*) and trial and error. There were no coaches for the shotgun snap—I was just told to learn to do it, and I did. I developed a technique where I'd kind of dead arm the ball back to the QB—it went back slowly but accurately. There were too many mistakes if I tried to zip it back to the QB, and a mistake usually meant a fumble or a sack. Yeah, I was nervous about it in practice, let alone trying it in a game. I drilled and drilled on it before and during practice. We didn't use it in game 3 for the NY Jets, which was an ugly loss. But we did plan to use it, live, against the Cardinals in St. Louis, game 4.

One of those games I can never forget. We played at old Busch Stadium, noon (Central Time) kickoff. We planned to use the new shotgun formation in this game, but not sure when. The Cardinals went up 7-0 in the second quarter. We got the ball and started our drive, and hit third and long, an obvious passing situation. The call was for shotgun formation, and I ran the play onto the field into the huddle. We came up to the line, where I surveyed the defense and made my pass-blocking calls to the rest of the line. I settled over the ball, balanced in a 3-point stance, meaning my right arm extended on the ball, my left cocked on my knee and ready to pass block after I snapped. Randy Wright, our backup QB, was in the game, Dickey out with some injury. As he went through his pre-snap cadence, the Cardinals defense shifted, showing blitz, and I yelled out the blocking adjustments. This meant I would have to snap the ball, shotgun style, with my right hand, and almost simultaneously step and turn toward my right to reach a linebacker who was shooting the gap outside my right shoulder. A tough block to make off a regular snap—much tougher off a shotgun snap where I had to finish the snap of the ball before moving to the block.

Wright yelled out the count, I snapped the ball and lunged over to block the blitzing linebacker. As I blocked him, and we fell to the ground, I heard a huge roar from the crowd. What did that mean?! On the ground, I rolled to look back at our QB, and all I could see was

Randy running *after* the ball, which was hopping along the ground toward our own end zone. *Shit!* I must have snapped it over his head in my lunge to make the block.

As the Cardinal defenders closed in on Randy, he finally, in desperation, just kicked the damn ball out of our end zone, soccer style, giving up the safety. I looked over to the sideline, where I knew I was heading, and could already feel the heat coming off Coach Gregg. I trotted over, nothing to say. He glared at me. But we both knew, and I *really* knew, that the shotgun was part of our game plan, and that I'd better be ready to go back out there and execute it again— and again—and again—successfully. No time for pity or excuses in the NFL. You made a mistake, you correct it, forget it, and execute. Which is what I did.

My first "live" shotgun snap was my only really bad shotgun snap—for the rest of the season, we ran the formation and I became pretty good at it; it became routine. But the first one, I'll always remember. Oh, and the Cardinals went on to beat us . . . badly. My mistake didn't help, but it was not a close game. And there you have it: my most embarrassing moment in the NFL, in front of 50,000 live fans and a regional TV audience. In a rather ironic twist, I always associate that moment with the high school game against our archrival, where I lofted the punt snap over our punter's head. When I am asked about my most embarrassing moments in life, these two spring to mind, standing out against all the *other* embarrassing moments.

Those of you with good NFL memories, remember that the 1985 Chicago Bears were not only good, but also eventually won that year's Super Bowl. And their defense was not just good, but has been called by many one of the best defenses of all time. The Bears offense was pretty good, but their defense was a terror. Offenses did not know how to block the complex defensive schemes introduced by Buddy Ryan, their defensive coordinator. Called the "46 Defense," it was an aggressive blitzing style designed to keep the offense completely on its heels, dictating tempo and play calling by attacking so ferociously that the offensive team was basically *defending* against the Bears defense. And the Bears had the perfect group of players to execute the madness of Ryan. Big and fast defensive linemen, embodied by Dan Hampton (the "Danimal") and Richard Dent. And one of the best middle linebackers ever to play the game, Mike Singletary. Defensive backs not afraid to play one-on-one coverage while the rest of the team was swarming the quarterback from all angles. They got better and better as the year progressed, more complicated yet more aggressive. On virtually every play, the Bears would rush more defenders than there were blockers, the idea being to overrun the offense. And it usually worked.

This scheme was an offensive lineman's worst nightmare. In most NFL defenses, one or two of the five offensive linemen would be "uncovered," meaning no defender was lined up directly over him. In those schemes, the uncovered lineman would check for a linebacker blitz, then help out the other linemen on passing plays. But with the Bears, every lineman was covered. Plus, we knew that there would usually be one or two or more blitzing linebackers, and they could come from any direction.

As for the center, the Bears would usually line up a defensive tackle, often the Danimal, over the snapping arm of the center, in my case my right arm. The reason was to gain a half-second advantage while my snapping arm was following through. The Danimal would slam into my right side and be halfway past me before I could get my right arm up and useful. Because my right guard was usually preoccupied with his own defensive tackle or linebacker blitzing, I couldn't get any help from my guard.

We prepared all week, or tried to prepare. We put in special plays designed to take advantage of the defense's "weaknesses," trying to use the blitzing aggressiveness to our advantage. Didn't work. We were overwhelmed. Our quarterback hardly had 2 seconds before a Bear, or Bears, were all over him. Running the ball was futile, because they usually had eight defenders charging the line, and Singletary rarely missed a tackle. Our "special" plays worked once or twice, but the offense could never get anything going. One-on-one vs. the

Danimal . . . I felt like I was chasing *him* as he'd whiz by me after our QB. And since Dickey, as noted before, wasn't very mobile, it was a very, *very* long afternoon. Actually *two* long afternoons, since we had to play them twice. And the results were similar . . . both times.

The Bears that year also introduced a young defensive tackle named William Perry. Due to his size and shape (maybe 6 feet, 320 pounds) he became known, well-known, as "Refrigerator" Perry. But for a man his size, he didn't move like a refrigerator—far from it. He was quick on his feet and tough to block.

Now, with the storied rivalry between the Bears and Packers, any opportunity by either team to punish, embarrass, or "show up" the other team was taken. Coach Mike Ditka, in our first game that season, came up with a unique form of humiliation. He put the 320-pound Refrigerator in the *offensive* backfield, down on the goal line. None of us were sure what was going on as we watched from the sideline. Why was he lined up in the backfield with Walter Payton, on our 3-yard line? The Bears snapped the ball, and in a blur, with a 3-yard running start, we saw Perry slam into our 225-pound linebacker and literally flatten him into the turf, with Payton stepping in for a touchdown behind him. First time we'd seen that, maybe a first in the NFL. Our linebacker could hardly get up. The Bears celebrated.

Soon after, the Bears were *back* at our goal line, same formation with Perry in the backfield. We were cringing even *before* the snap, hard to watch what we thought was going to happen again to our poor linebacker. But Ditka had a different flavor of humiliation in mind this time. When the ball was snapped, it was handed to Perry, who with a full head of steam crashed into and through our defense like a bowling ball through pins. *Touchdown!* He gave the ball an enormous spike . . . and the humiliation was complete. Our only consolation, if any, was that the Bears were humiliating almost everyone that year.

In our second Bears game that year, this time at home in Green Bay, it was more of the same. Their defense had our offense on the run most of the day. It felt like they had 13 or 14 guys on the field. And then the dreaded goal line offense, with Perry in the backfield again. We waited for the inevitable, but it didn't come. No, actually, this time they faked the run, Perry crashed into the end zone, turned, and they *passed* to him for a touchdown. Now that was just plain rude. But so went the rivalry. And, yes, we lost again.

The first nine games of our season were shaping up like the first half of the last season. We started slowly, digging ourselves a hole with a 3-6 record. It was frustrating to be past the midpoint of the season again with only a small chance to make the playoffs. We undertook to turn it around in the second half of the season. One of our bright spots was hosting New Orleans in Milwaukee (we had three "home" games in Milwaukee each year then). It was a great fall day in Wisconsin. Arriving at the stadium at 9 or 10 in the morning, the sweet smell of brats and onions cooking in beer wafted over the parking lot and stadium. Even with my shotgun and passing down duties, I was still also used as the extra blocking tight end on short yardage and goal line plays. I was in the game a lot, with multiple responsibilities. For this week's game, apparently one of the coaches remembered my extraordinary (?) pass-catching ability, from my TD catch in the Lions game in the previous season. For the Saints, we actually designed a play where I would be the *intended* (not accidental) receiver in a goal line situation. We practiced it a few times during the week before. I'd catch the ball in practice, laughing, and practice my spiking technique . . . never really expecting we'd actually call the play in the game.

But in the first half, there we were down on the Saints' goal line, the 3-yard line. We were winning only 3-0, and having trouble scoring. I was sent in as the extra tight end, for our "big" goal line offense. In came the play—*my* pass play! On the play, my job was to line up at right end, block hard for a second, then slip out toward the left half of the end zone while all the rest of the offense went to the right. The ball was snapped, I slammed into the defender across from me, disentangled myself, and ran toward the left half of the end zone. I realized as I turned back to the QB, who was rolling to the right, that the play fake had worked to perfection—I was wide open in the end zone, no defenders paying any attention to me. Dickey lofted a very gentle pass right to me, and this time I actually had a split second to think about catching it (or dropping it!). As the ball settled into my hands, the crowd roared. *Touchdown!* This time, I was ready. No atomic spike for me—no, I ran through the end zone and executed a little over-the-shoulder-behind-the-back flip of the ball, like I'd done it many times. After the yelling stopped, I secured the ball, touchdown #2, and it also sits in my trophy case at home. Coach Gregg again thought this whole scene was quite funny, laughing on the sideline as I trotted over. We went on to beat the Saints that day, in what was truly a fun day to be playing football in the NFL.

After beating the Saints, we had won two straight games and were regaining our confidence. Our next game was out in Los Angeles, against the Rams. Strange to be playing a game in late November on a warm sunny day, but such is the travel life of an NFL schedule. The Rams were good in 1985, and in fact, made it to the playoffs until they were shut out by the eventual Super Bowl champion Bears. I was playing my usual multiple roles in this game: shotgun center, extra tight end, special teams. Toward the end of the first half, I was playing center as we were trying to score before halftime. We were losing because we had given up two touchdowns to the Rams on long kickoff returns of 98 and 86 yards. Doing that once was bad, but *twice* in one half? Horrible. We were driving down the field. The Rams' nose tackle at the time was a big guy, who was bull-rushing hard right over me. On one play, he brought his fist up into my chin, knocking my head back as the play continued. When I went back to the huddle, I noticed I had a fair amount of blood dripping through my chinstrap onto my jersey. He had opened up a good cut on my chin, which I ignored until we went into the locker room at halftime. There, the team doctor cleaned off my split open chin and decided I needed stitches to hold it together. Halftime is short, so no time for any local painkiller—he just loaded up his needle and put in a few stitches, and I was ready to go for the second half. Which turned out poorly for us, as the Rams scored 13 in the fourth quarter to put the game away.

I have talked a little about the Green Bay community and their love of their Packers. I like to say there are only three "passions" in Green Bay: cheese, deer hunting, and the Green Bay Packers. And not in that order. The community loves its Packers, and we loved them back. One weekend we were hosting Tampa Bay in Green Bay for a divisional game. It was December 1, the Sunday after a late-November Thanksgiving. At Thanksgiving, Cindy and I opened up our home not just to our families (we had brothers and sisters and Cindy's parents in for the game), but also to several "stray" offensive linemen and our kicker. We must have had 20 people there, cooked two 20-pound-plus turkeys, and stood back and watched a frenzy of consumption that was mind-bending. Remember, these were 275-pound offensive linemen, at Thanksgiving. I don't think we had any leftovers. Our family guests watched in wonder and amazement. It was one of our best Thanksgivings ever.

Anyway, that following Sunday, Tampa Bay came to town. So did a snowstorm. And not just *any* snowstorm, but snow coming down hard and fast. We lived in a typical Green Bay suburban neighborhood and knew our neighbors, and they knew us. A teenager across the street babysat our kids for us. We were welcomed there and treated like family. We had seen the weather predictions, but when I woke up Sunday morning at home (Coach Gregg actually let us stay at home the night before a game in Green Bay—I suppose it was a function of "how much trouble could you really get into in Green Bay?"), there was already almost a foot of snow on the ground. Of course, I had to drive over to the stadium early to get ready for the game, and it looked like my day would start with shoveling the driveway. But then I heard a buzzing noise outside, and went out to see what was going on. Unasked, one of my neighbors was out there snow-blowing my driveway! I went over to thank him—he said of course he was clearing my driveway—had to be sure I made it to the game on time. I love Green Bay!

I did make it to the game on time, and the snow kept coming.

Of course, our fans loved it. They just added another layer of clothing, cleaned off the aluminum seats, and settled in for a Green Bay Packer afternoon. We loved it too—Packer weather! Tampa Bay—not so much. It was snowing so hard that the field was and stayed completely white. The yard lines were obliterated no matter how furiously they were swept off. Players were skidding and sliding all over the place, but we had put extra-long cleats in our shoes and so slipped and slid less than Tampa Bay, who really just didn't want any part of the whole mess. And it showed—we beat them soundly and had a fun afternoon doing it.

After the game, we offensive linemen did some running belly sliding on the field in the snow, reveling in the weather, Lambeau Field, and the win. At the time, it went down as the snowiest NFL game in history, and I think it may still be.

I have only talked about my injury history in the NFL in passing, so it might be worth a clinical listing of my injuries during my 6-year career, in no particular order:

- multiple sprained ankles, usually just re-taped tighter and kept playing
- sprained right knee, missed two weeks of practice
- pulled hamstring, missed several days of practice
- multiple finger and wrist jams and sprains—just tape them up and play on
- concussions and "bell ringers"—multiple, during practice and games, though no "diagnosed" concussions. At this time in the NFL, a diagnosed concussion basically meant being knocked unconscious. Other head injuries usually resulted in a play or two on the sidelines, the crack of an ammonia capsule under your nose to "clear your head," the question "how many fingers am I holding up" from the trainer, and back in the game.
- chin gash with several stitches
- severe deep bruise to the quadriceps, limiting practice but not missing practice

- partial shoulder dislocation, where I was offered a painkilling injection before the game, but I declined. When I used my shoulder in the game, the pain was excruciating, but I didn't trust a painkilling injection.
- strained lower back a couple times, which "only" hurt when I would get into my football stance. No missed practice time, just pain.

These are the injuries I remember, and I was extremely fortunate compared to most of my teammates. The fact that I had played my position on the line through college and 6 years in the NFL without ever having surgery made me an anomaly. I watched many other players experience much worse. And we all understood that any play in any game or practice could be your last, but that thought was pushed completely out of your head. It might happen to someone else, but it couldn't happen to me. That is simply the mentality we all had to bring on the field every single day.

The win in the "Snow Bowl" kept our slim playoff hopes alive for another week, with a 6-7 record. But in came another good playoff team, the Miami Dolphins, and on a cold clear day at Lambeau they pretty much finished us off, beating us 34-24. Dan Marino threw 5 touchdown passes that afternoon. After the game, we knew our season was effectively over with 8 losses, and no chance for the playoffs. That didn't matter to Coach Gregg, who reminded us all in a not-so-gentle way that we were professionals, and by God, we had two games left against division rivals, and by God, we were going to work our asses off the next two weeks, and by God, we were going to finish strong and win.

And we did.

The Lions needed a win to keep their playoff hopes alive, and they had us at home in front of an always-hostile crowd. Despite a fast start, we fought back and beat them in a close game, sending their record to 7-8, and ending *their* playoff hopes. It may be hard to understand, but in many ways it was one of our more satisfying wins because we knocked one of our hated division rivals out of the race, in front of *their* fans.

Our last game of the season was in Tampa Bay, against a poor Buccaneer team, on December 22. Now, that was just before Christmas, of course. We all knew this was our last game of the season. But Coach Gregg had already made plans of his own. Back a few games, when we were still in the playoff race, he had made a decision that we would spend the week before the Tampa Bay game *in* Florida. *In Florida?* The idea was to get down there as a team away from any distractions and get ready to play. Now, had a playoff spot been on the line, I think we all would have bought into the idea of leaving our families for the week before Christmas to get ready. But as it was, we were *not* in the playoffs. And none of us really wanted to go to Florida for a week to practice right before Christmas. So somehow, I got "nominated" by a few of my teammates to ask Coach Gregg if he would reconsider the decision. I suppose they thought I "knew him" better since he'd been my coach for 6 years. Anyway, I did knock on Coach Gregg's office door and asked the question. His eyes lit up, and in almost a growl he said, "The decision is final. We're going, and we are going to win." And that was that.

We spent a lovely week holed up at the LA Dodgers training facility at Vero Beach, working out and sweating under the hot Florida sun. And a frustrated group we were when we took the field in Tampa Bay. And we took it out on the Buccaneers, finishing our disappointing season with a win, but again with a very unsatisfying 8-8 record. We climbed on the plane and flew back to cold Green Bay, my sixth NFL season over. I had no idea (again) what the next year would bring. And I had no idea that I'd just played in my last NFL game, and last football game. Period.

After breaking for the holidays with my family, we were back in Green Bay, in our rental house on Sequoia Lane. Cindy had resumed her MBA courses "remotely," meaning she was taking her final MBA classes at the University of Wisconsin—Oshkosh, about 90 minutes from Green Bay. That always gave me some "quality time" with my two small children, and they had me outnumbered, for sure. We might go over to the local Shakey's Pizza buffet, where the kids ate all they wanted for a penny a pound. Even though young, Lauren and Hudson made them pay for *that* bargain. Cindy eventually completed her graduate work that winter of 1986, earning her MBA from Xavier via UW Oshkosh.

In the meantime, what about my NFL career, law school, the Packers, life, etc.? I still felt I could play, and wanted to play, at least another year with Green Bay. At 28, I was still in my prime as an offensive lineman. At the same time, through careful money management and living within our means, through savings and deferrals of my NFL contract payments combined with the "severance plan" that became part of the Collective Bargaining Agreement benefits for veterans like me, we had saved or deferred enough money to get me through three years of law school with a family of four. I had contacted Harvard again to inquire about the possibility for another year's deferral so I could play another season—and Harvard said yes. After discussing it with Cindy, I set an appointment in January 1986 to meet with Coach Gregg to discuss my future in the NFL, with Green Bay.

In the meantime, off-season in Green Bay was a busy time for the few Packer players who stayed in town (winter in Green Bay?!). The Packers sponsored a Green Bay Packers "speakers' bureau," where various organizations, like schools, civic associations, and others, could arrange to have a player come and speak to their organization. And we players would get a small stipend from the Packers (maybe a couple hundred dollars) to make the appearance. I signed up and did as many as I could, probably 20 or so during the off-season. I spoke in front of small groups (20–30) and large crowds (several hundred). I was in tiny towns and big cities around Wisconsin. I spoke in all kinds of venues, from school gyms to school cafeterias to restaurants. My comments were usually built around the same general outline—my journey to the NFL, the hard work and discipline it took to get there, along with the timely help from people noted in this book. If speaking to kids, I always talked about the importance of studying hard and being good in school—things that helped *me* make it in the NFL. Two particularly memorable events stand out from the off-season travels.

One trip was an invite to speak up in Sister Bay, Wisconsin. "Up" as in north of Green Bay, in the dead of winter. We got a babysitter, and Cindy came along for this engagement. Sister Bay was supposed to be a lovely place. And it was, though harder to appreciate perhaps on a cold winter night. We drove into the tiny town, slowly looking for the address for my appearance. Found it—a bowling alley. We went inside, and there were gathered about 30 or 40 of the best Packer fans anywhere, who came out on a cold winter night to meet me, an offensive lineman, share some food, hear some stories, get some autographs. After I was finished, they presented me with a beautiful painting by a local artist of a boat in the Sister Bay harbor. We still have that painting, and it reminds us always of the way the people of Sister Bay warmed our hearts that cold night.

The other engagement of note involved a drive through a typical Wisconsin winter storm to a church near a small town. I arrived along with others in the snow as the parking lot filled up. We convened in the basement of the church, seated around a large rectangle of folding tables in the room. Dinner was "potluck," featuring a delicious stew that we all served ourselves before we were seated. Before eating, the group leader stood to kick off the evening: "Thanks for coming out, and thanks to Blake Moore of the Packers for joining us tonight. Before our prayer and our meal, I also want to thank [Jim], who hit the deer with his pickup truck that you are enjoying in your stew tonight." Yes, that's right, we were enjoying "roadkill" stew! But it was *fresh* roadkill. I do love Packer fans.

We players who stayed around for the off-season also organized a number of charity basketball games. We traveled all over Wisconsin playing in towns from Menomonie to Tomahawk, from Ashland to Iron Mountain. We traveled to little communities where it seemed the entire population turned out to watch a few Green Bay Packers play basketball, and get some autographs. But we were *their* Packers, and they loved us.

My meeting with Coach Gregg arrived—time to figure out my future in the NFL. After being released/cut by the Bengals, Cindy and I had decided that we *never* wanted to put our family in that kind of uncertain position again. So I had a fairly simple proposition for Coach Gregg. I wanted to play another year for Green Bay, and for him, but I needed a guaranteed contract for 1986. I explained to him that I was financially situated to go through Harvard Law School, had the three years set up financially, but that I wasn't willing to take the risk of "losing" one of those years if I deferred Harvard for another year, then did *not* make the Packers team in August. Then I would have been out a year of pay, and be short a year for law school.

Coach Gregg understood and told me he wanted me to stay and play, that he thought I would make the team. On the other hand, he said he could not guarantee me a spot, nor were the Packers in a position to "guarantee" my contract, even for a year. (Remember, NFL contracts are not guaranteed—you have to make the team to get paid.) In the end, I thanked him but told him that the best thing for my family was to retire and go to law school in that case. I was not willing to risk the uncertainty involved in trying for another season. He understood, and we decided to hold off on my retirement announcement until early spring, but he knew my plans so he could plan accordingly in the off-season.

And there it was. The end of my NFL, and football, career. The suddenness of its end is inherent to the game. I can't say I went out with a bang, but I did retire on my own terms, something that I had vowed to do after being cut by the Bengals. I continued to participate in the off-season Packer player activities, as my retirement wasn't public or official yet. Cindy and I began making plans for our next life adventure—moving to Boston and my attending Harvard Law School. I called Harvard to let them know I would be attending in the fall of 1986, class of '89. We kept ourselves very busy during the long Green Bay winter.

I turned to the one remaining "football" goal I still had to handle:

my weight. I was a robust 275 pounds, and I knew from watching other players retire, and seeing other retired players, that 275 pounds while you are playing is *very* different than 275 pounds when you are retired and 40. And I had told myself as I was putting the weight on, that someday it would have to come off. As soon as I had that conversation with Coach Gregg and made the decision to retire, so too came the decision to drop the weight. How much? Well, 60 pounds seemed the "right" amount, which would take me back to what I weighed when I started college, and before I intentionally started putting on the weight. My methodology was not too scientific, nor doctor- or drug-assisted. Once I decided what my goal was, I cut my diet approximately in half, from 5,000–6,000 calories a day to 2,000–3,000 calories a day. I didn't so much change what I ate, just the quantity. For example, no more gallon of milk per day. And my exercise changed from a regimen that was focused on heavy weight lifting and power, to a more aerobic, calorie-burning routine. I ran more, played racquetball, basketball, and pretty much stopped lifting weights.

The results were dramatic. I like to say "the first 30 pounds were easy," and they were. That came off in a month or two. During my time in the NFL I didn't need many really nice dress clothes, like suits. Cindy had bought me one very nice dark navy pin-striped suit that I used for most of my playing days—it was a 52 extra long, with a waist of 42. After the first 30 pounds we had the entire suit resized, and it still fit OK in my shoulders. Over the next several months, as I approached my goal of 60 pounds, we had it resized again. Finally, at the last meeting with the tailor, he told me that the back pants pockets were going to run together into one large pocket. That's when I knew the suit was history, but also that I had nearly achieved my "return to normalcy."

My teammates in Green Bay were beginning to suspect something was up as I dropped from 275 to 250, and then lower. I was looking skinny. Finally, around April, the Packers and I agreed to release the announcement. It was just a little article in the Green Bay paper sports section, maybe with a head shot photo that noted my decision to retire and attend Harvard Law School.

That was it. We packed up our belongings from our rental home in April 1986, loaded up the minivan, and set off on our new life adventure. For the first time in my life, the *rest* of my life would not involve football. I would play no more, and I never really seriously entertained the notion that I'd coach football or be involved in that capacity. And though that has remained true—I have never again been directly involved in football in any way—it is also true that my life in many ways still reflects through a pigskin prism. The lessons learned, the failures, the successes, the competition, the ability to do something that most people thought I would never do, the discipline, the teamwork, the drive—all these things have been with me through football and during my professional and personal life after football. My life has not been defined by football, but much of what I have been able to achieve and do is attributable to, and a reflection of, my football career and lessons from the field. Through a pigskin prism.

Epilogue

AS WE DROVE out of Green Bay on that cold April day in 1986, I really had no idea what my future would hold. I knew I was going to one of the best law schools in the world, and I figured I'd be "a lawyer" for a while, but my long-term goals did *not* include being a lawyer for the rest of my life. My family was my priority, and the Harvard law degree should ensure the kind of financial security I wanted us to have.

We bought the middle level of a traditional Cambridge, Massachusetts, triple-decker—1,300 square feet, one bathroom for the four of us to share. About half the size of the place we'd rented in Green Bay. I registered for classes, had my class photo taken (wearing my Packers helmet), and set up my study table in front of a large picture window looking across Maple Avenue to the little playground there. Most of my awake time the next 2½ years was spent in classes, at my study desk, or across the street in that playground with Lauren and/or Hudson. It's funny, but I never had any doubts that I'd handle law school, and Harvard, just fine. In fact, after the intensity of the NFL, the demands of law school were actually not so bad. Most of my classmates, on the other hand, were totally stressed out and afraid they'd fail. Cindy asked me at one point during the fall if I wasn't maybe watching too much NFL football on TV. I probably was, but when my first semester grades came in, I did just fine.

That first football season as an observer wasn't always easy. It was the first fall since fourth grade that I wasn't actually *playing* football.

And I did miss the competition, the intensity, the black and white of beating my man, winning and losing on a Sunday afternoon. And I realized while missing this that the rest of my career, whatever I did, would not match my NFL experience in that regard. That wasn't a disappointment, but rather a recognition of what I had in the NFL, the rare air I was in while playing there.

I did successfully graduate from Harvard Law School, and we all moved out to live and work and thrive in San Diego, California. A beautiful city and wonderful place to raise our family. I worked at a large law firm for a few years, then was recruited as general counsel for an investment management firm in San Diego, where I spent the next 11 years of my career. I eventually moved out of a legal role into a business leadership role, which I enjoyed. I also found I loved the investment management business, because it is very competitive and success requires better-than-average results, year after year. Closest thing to the NFL I'd found.

Our company was bought by the large insurance company, Allianz, in 2001, and in 2004, they asked me to become the CEO of one of their investment management businesses based out of New York City. Our kids had grown up in San Diego, happily, and were both in college, so away we went again, this time on our New York City adventure. Again, to do something I'd never done before, yet again, full of confidence that I could do anything. After 6 years running various business units in New York, I was recruited to a division of a large Canadian investment management firm, and so in 2011, we were off to Toronto (ironically, the city where Coach Gregg coached the Argonauts immediately before joining the Bengals). The work I do as an executive is, in many ways, completely different than anything I ever did on the football field. But time and again, I find myself using lessons learned on the practice field, in the locker room, in the weight room, and from game day, in the work that I do in business. Indeed, much of my life still reflects through a pigskin prism. I don't define myself as a football player, but in many ways, football continues to define me.

CPSIA information can be obtained at www.ICGtesting.com
Printed in the USA
LVOW10s0916011014

406736LV00002B/340/P